If you have enjoyed this book and would like to receive a free catalog of Self-Counsel titles, please write to the appropriate address below:

Self-Counsel Press Inc.
1704 North State Street
Bellingham, WA 98225

Self-Counsel Press
4 Bram Court
Brampton, ON L6W 3R6

Or visit us on the World Wide Web at *www.self-counsel.com*

Other books in the Start & Run series:
Bed & Breakfast
Bookkeeping Business
Catering Business
Coffee Bar
Consulting Business
Copywriting Business
Craft Business
Creative Services Business
Desktop Publishing Business
ESL Teaching Business
Event Planning Business
Gift Basket Business
Handyman Business
Home Cleaning Business
Home Daycare
Landscaping Business
Restaurant Business
Rural Computer Consulting Business
Tour Guiding Business

START & RUN A

Retail Business

James E. Dion and Ted Topping

- Create a competitive niche business
- Deliver on-brand service to your target customers
- Harness the full potential of today's retail technology

Includes retail spreadsheets and checklists on a CD-ROM

Self-Counsel Press

BUSINESS SERIES

START AND RUN A RETAIL BUSINESS

James E. Dion and Ted Topping

Self-Counsel Press
(a division of)
International Self-Counsel Press Ltd.
USA   Canada

Self-Counsel Press acknowledges the financial support of the Government of Canada through the Book Publishing Industry Development Program (BPIDP) for our publishing activities.

Printed in Canada.

First edition: 1998; Reprinted: 1998; 2000; 2002; 2004; 2005

Second edition: 2007

Library and Archives Canada Cataloguing in Publication

Dion, Jim
    Start and run a retail business / by Jim Dion and Ted Topping. — 2nd ed.

    Accompanied by a CD-ROM.
    ISBN-13: 978-1-55180-723-2
    ISBN-10: 1-55180-723-8

    1. Retail trade — Management. 2. New business enterprises.
I. Topping, Ted II. Title.

HF5429.D56 2006   658.8'7   C2006-904908-4

ANCIENT FOREST
FRIENDLY

Self-Counsel Press
(a division of)
International Self-Counsel Press Ltd.

1704 North State Street
Bellingham, WA 98225
USA

1481 Charlotte Road
North Vancouver, BC V7J 1H1
Canada

CONTENTS

CHECKLISTS

FIGURES

SAMPLES

WORKSHEETS

NOTICE TO READERS

ACKNOWLEDGMENTS

Although our names appear on the cover of this book, we gratefully acknowledge the people who have helped us along the way.

Jim Dion acknowledges the contribution of Stefania Pinton, Senior HR Partner at Dionco Inc. in Chicago. Stefania is an expert in training design and development, and she brings an in-depth knowledge of the retail industry gained through years of experience with a large international company.

Ted Topping acknowledges the contribution of Tuija Seipell, a communications and marketing expert and his partner at Creative Insights Inc. in Vancouver. With her clear and precise logic, Tuija often helped us step back from the trees so that we could again see the forest when we were originally writing this book.

We also need to thank Terri Lee Birker, an owner-operated retailer in Kelowna, British Columbia, who read the first draft of our original text and offered comments that we found invaluable.

Last but not least, thank you to the many people who taught *us* along the way.

PREFACE TO THE SECOND EDITION

When Self-Counsel Press asked us to create a new edition of this book, we welcomed the chance to tweak some of the little things in the first edition that had been nagging at us for years. The technology chapter, in particular, needed an update to reflect the incredible evolution of computers and the Internet that we have witnessed in recent years.

As huge as the changes in technology have been, however, they pale in comparison to the change in customers' expectations that we have seen over the same period.

This is not something that you hear owner-operated retailers talk about very often. That could be because many are stuck in the "good old days" of 35 years ago when manufacturers, wholesalers and retailers held all the power in the marketplace. They could basically design, manufacture, distribute, promote, and sell whatever products they wished. Customers had little choice but to buy on those terms.

The Internet has changed all that. In addition to e-commerce, it has brought a new version of "power to the people." At an ever-increasing rate, the balance of power is shifting toward the customer — which means that nothing about the retail business can ever be the same.

While this new power structure is a problem for some existing retailers, it can be a significant competitive advantage for an owner-operated retailer who is just starting out. That is why we are adding an entire chapter to the book. It will help you to stand on the other side of the counter and to see your business from the perspective of your customers.

This is the only way that you can even hope to give people what they want. And that is the one thing that will make your business a success.

Jim Dion and Ted Topping

INTRODUCTION

If you are thinking about opening a retail business, you have found the right book. *Start and Run a Retail Business* will provide you with a real-world view of retail and lead you step by step through the process of making an informed decision about opening a store. We recommend strongly that you do make an informed decision, because being an owner-operated retailer is not an easy job today.

As recently as 35 years ago, owner-operated retailers had very little competition and it was relatively easy to make a profit. Year after year, they enjoyed 20 to 25 percent growth, which meant they could afford to make a few mistakes and simply sweep them under the carpet.

If you are a baby boomer or older, perhaps you recall the days when Main Street in every city and town in North America boasted a thriving community of owner-operated retailers. Unfortunately, most of those stores are now gone. One at a time, they became another statistic confirming the power of the efficient distribution systems and huge advertising budgets of the large national and international retailers.

Because the retail business has changed, this book is very different from the one we would have written 35 years ago. Back then, we would have devoted our entire book to the basics of retail and left you standing in a just-opened store wondering what to do next. You probably would have survived though, and perhaps even prospered.

If we were to give you that same level of guidance today, you probably would not survive, and you certainly would not prosper. For that reason, we have devoted just one chapter to the basics of retail and from there, we take you far beyond opening day. Our plan is to leave you standing in a store that has been operating for two years, knowing exactly what you are going to do next.

In the broadest sense, a retail business can take many forms. However, this book deals only with what most people think of when they hear the term *retail* — a traditional retail business in a traditional store location, where customers come to purchase items from an inventory of products that the retailer has bought in order to sell.

This book does *not* deal with any of the other forms of retail, those we refer to as nontraditional retail businesses. These include selling —

- by catalog, whether in paper or electronic form, where customers order a product by mail, telephone, fax, or email, or directly from a website;
- at a flea market or some other temporary location;
- door-to-door or on the street;
- over the telephone;
- through a direct-mail flyer;
- at a consumer or trade show; and
- through a TV or radio infomercial.

While there are similarities between traditional and nontraditional retail businesses, there are also significant differences. So significant, that you should put this book down if you want to start a nontraditional retail business. You will be able to find much better sources of information.

If you are thinking about opening a home-based business or an on-site service business, you should also put this book down. This book is about traditional retail businesses with both a store location and an inventory of products to sell, which does not apply to home-based and on-site service businesses.

We think it is important to tell you right at the outset that starting and running a *profitable* retail business is much more than a hobby or a part-time job. Thirty-five years ago, you could probably have viewed it in those ways. Today, you will have no choice but to view it as a demanding career.

Most owner-operated retailers feel that they have a 24-hour-a-day, seven-day-a-week job. Their businesses are not necessarily open all of those hours, but their thoughts are usually back at the store. While you may be able to have a life outside of retail after two or three years in business, you must be willing to devote a huge amount of time to your business initially if you want to make it work.

You must also possess certain characteristics to enjoy the job. Ask yourself the following questions:

Are you a "people person"?	☐ Yes	☐ No
Do you truly respect people and always try to see something from another person's perspective?	☐ Yes	☐ No
Are you willing to rely on other people?	☐ Yes	☐ No
Do you take pride in helping others reach their goals?	☐ Yes	☐ No
Are you organized?	☐ Yes	☐ No
Do you enjoy attending to the smallest details?	☐ Yes	☐ No
Are you prepared to admit that you do not know everything?	☐ Yes	☐ No
Do you work well under the pressure of deadlines?	☐ Yes	☐ No

If you can truthfully answer yes to all these questions, you will probably enjoy running a retail business. If you cannot, then we believe you should proceed with extreme caution. Few people without these characteristics are successful owner-operated retailers. One of the things that we will be doing throughout the book is offering an extensive job description of an owner-operated retailer. Each chapter represents a different part of the job, and each part is important.

Learning to Be a Generalist

Many individuals spend their careers as specialists in one field or another. They know essentially one thing, and they know just about everything there is to know about it. As an owner-operated retailer, you cannot be a specialist and be successful. Rather, you must spend your career as a *generalist*. You will need to know an amazing amount about many things.

Your job as an owner-operated retailer will be something of a juggling act. You will stand in the store every day, trying to keep a large number of balls in the air. Each ball represents just one part of the total job you need to do. Since we were writing a book and not an encyclopedia, we decided to focus on the eight most important juggling balls and devote a chapter to each one:

- The basics of retail
- Merchandising
- Buying
- Human resources
- Sales management
- Technology
- Customer service
- The in-store experience

If you have ever seen a professional juggler, you will know that trying to keep just five balls in the air is a huge challenge. This will give you some idea of the challenge you face in starting and running a profitable retail business.

Just as important as what's in this book is what we have intentionally left out. We believe that you stand a good chance of starting and running a profitable retail business if you are prepared to follow the steps outlined in this book, learn your craft, and become a professional retailer. This means that you should not *also* try to become an accountant, lease negotiator, lawyer, store designer, advertising copywriter, retail trainer, technology specialist, website designer, or any of the *other* professions that your job as a retailer touches on.

Juggling those eight balls will give you more than enough to do. To run a profitable retail business, you will need to be clear on where your job should end and where the job of an outside professional should begin. Unfortunately, jobs such as negotiating leases and designing ads are things that amateurs can attempt to do. They may even be things that you would like to try. However, we believe that the more you dabble outside your job as a professional retailer, the less successful your business will be. If you cannot afford to use freelancers or outside professionals, you should proceed with extreme caution. The money you save may not be worth the time spent away from your job as a professional retailer.

How to Use This Book

Throughout this book, we have used easy-to-understand icons to help keep things clear. If you need to find something quickly, these icons in the margins should help you.

The **your job description** icon appears at the beginning of each chapter beside a list of specific skills and subjects you will need to master within that chapter's topic. Once you have read all eight chapters, you will have some valuable insight into the real-life job description of an owner-operated retailer. Under the best of circumstances, running a small business is something of a juggling act. You will need to understand all the various details in order to see the big picture.

your job description

The **where you want to go** icon indicates that you are reading a description of how your retail business should be operating about three years after you decide to start your business, and about two years after opening day. This icon represents you sailing peacefully on calm waters.

where you want to go

The icon for **that's a good idea** highlights a piece of information that will be useful to you at some point during the next three years. This icon is of a light going on as you connect with an idea that perhaps did not make much sense at first but is exactly the idea you need to use now or in the future.

that's a good idea

A word to the wise is designed to provide a gentle caution about a specific issue. This icon is of a fairly stern-looking owl warning you not to make a mistake when you could easily do something right the first time.

a word to the wise

Do the calculation takes you through a hands-on exercise. This could be anything from a simple calculation to a detailed budget. We have provided copies of the most important budget worksheets and checklists on the accompanying CD-ROM. You will rework these often if you decide to open a retail business, so you may want to print out several blank forms if you are completing these by hand. This icon is of a calculator posed to help you check if your business idea will work.

do the calculation

Put it to work indicates a section at the end of each chapter. We believe that you should pause when you see this icon to think through everything you have just read. You need to decide exactly what to do next — either forget the whole idea of opening a retail store or act on several specific issues. This icon is of a clipboard and a checklist that you can build into an action plan as you work through the book.

put it to work

In this book we try to paint a picture of where you want to go in the retail business. As we started to plan this book, we quickly realized that it could not follow a traditional how-to format. This would have required us to assume that all of our readers are starting from the same place and that we could systematically lead them through the process of opening a retail business.

Whether you have worked in retail all of your life or this is your first step into the business, we believe that you will be able to figure out where you are now. Once you know that, you should know how to begin work toward achieving the picture we have painted in **where you want to go**.

This will probably be at least a three-year process. You will spend year one doing everything it takes just to get the doors open. It will take six months to think through your business idea and arrange the necessary financing, and another six months to find a location, buy merchandise, hire sales associates, and so on.

And then comes opening day. As we will learn in Chapter 3, most retailers divide the year into two buying seasons. The spring season runs from February until July and the fall season runs from August until January. It is best to open your business at the start of one of these two seasons, in either February or August. This will give you the maximum time to sell the merchandise you bought at the outset and a full season of sales results on which to plan your second year.

Realistically, you will spend year two (the first year your store is open) operating your business largely by trial and error. You will discover all of the ways that your business in reality is different from the business you originally pictured in your mind. This is normal and you should expect it to be this way. The trick will be to learn from your mistakes and get things right in the following year.

If you do, you should then be able to spend year three (the second year your store is open) doing things much the way we describe them in this book. You may not actually be sailing peacefully on calm waters, but you should at least have things under control and be focusing most of your efforts on expanding and shaping the business into what you want it to become.

The following timeline illustrates the three-year process for opening a retail business.

1
THE BASICS OF RETAIL

This part of your job includes:

your job description

- Buying an item at wholesale and selling it for more than you paid for it

- Understanding the ways that the many variables affect your net-profit line

- Preparing a pro forma profit and loss statement for your new business

- Adding value to the products you sell by adopting a best-service strategy

- Developing a strategic framework, including your unique secret weapon

- Identifying and studying your three most important direct competitors

- Developing a clear vision of your business by picturing it in your mind

- Conveying your strategic message through your store location

- Conveying your strategic message through your store design and layout

- Conveying your strategic message through your media advertising

where you want to go

Understanding the Six Rights of Retail

The basic premise of the retail business is simple — you buy an item at wholesale and sell it for more than you paid for it. Unfortunately, the things in life that seem simple are often very challenging. And in this case, selling an item involves getting *six* things right. We call these the "six rights of retail":

> To be successful, you need to have the right item, in the right place, at the right time, in the right quantity, at the right price, with the right service.

We do not take credit for inventing the six rights of retail. They have challenged retailers for years, defining the business and demonstrating just how much more there is to retail than selling an item for more than you paid for it. For a start, you need to sell it with enough gross profit to pay all of your expenses and leave a net profit.

Your Profit and Loss Statement

The following is a retail income statement in its most basic form. It could describe your business as it will look three years from now:

Net sales	$ 800,000
− Cost of goods sold	440,000
Gross profit (also called "maintained margin")	360,000
− Expenses (also called "SG&A")	340,000
Net profit	$ 20,000

The top line shows net sales, the total amount that you received from customers. You subtract from that the *cost of goods sold*, the total amount you paid to buy the merchandise that customers bought from you, including any freight costs. This gives your gross profit, also called your *maintained margin*.

From that gross profit figure, you subtract all of your expenses, known in retail as *selling, general, and administration* (SG&A), and you are left with your net profit, the total amount remaining at the end of the year. Hopefully, this is a positive number.

By separating the expenses into various standard categories and calculating the percentage of net sales that each category represents, you produce a *profit and loss statement* that tells you more about the operation of your business. Sample 1 shows a typical profit and loss statement. (We have included a blank version of this as an Excel spreadsheet on the CD-ROM.)

If you are not familiar with the retail business, the net profit figure in this sample may come as a surprise. Like many people, you may have had a vague notion that retailers simply double the wholesale price of an item and pocket the difference.

In reality, this sample profit and loss statement is quite typical of the retail business today. For running an $800,000 business, this owner-operated retailer made a net profit of only $20,000, or 2.5 percent of sales.

If you look closely at the figures in Sample 1, you will notice that some expenses are *fixed expenses*. For example, the cost of utilities would not change if the store did $600,000 in sales rather than $800,000, or $1 million rather than $800,000.

Other expenses are not fixed, but neither do they vary by the same percentage in either direction as the sales figures. For example, the cost of supplies would change if sales decreased or increased by 25 percent, but the change would be *less* than 25 percent.

By examining these expenses carefully, you can determine the *breakeven sales figure* for the business. This is the amount of sales needed to cover the expenses incurred in running the business. It does not include the cost of goods sold. After your first full year of operation, this is a number that your accountant will be able to calculate easily. Until then, you will need to use an estimate.

Sample 2 shows three profit and loss scenarios, indicating how expenses can vary with sales. A careful examination of these scenarios should help you understand the ways that expenses can vary with sales.

They also illustrate three very important realities of the retail business. First, you need a certain amount in sales just to cover your expenses and make a profit. We have no idea what the breakeven point will be for your particular business, but we do know that calculating and understanding this figure will be critical to your success.

Second, once you get past the breakeven point, sales increases affect the net profit line at an increasing rate. In Sample 2, a 25 percent increase in sales from $800,000 to $1,000,000 resulted in a 240 percent increase in net profit.

SAMPLE 1
PROFIT AND LOSS STATEMENT

		Amount	Percentage of net sales	
	Net sales	$800,000	100.0%	The total amount that you received from customers. Does not include sales taxes, which are sent directly to the government.
(minus)	**Cost of goods sold**	440,000	55.0%	The total amount you paid to buy the merchandise that customers bought from you, including any freight costs.
(equals)	**Gross profit**	360,000	45.0%	This is the amount of money that you have in order to pay your bills. What is left over will become your net profit.
(minus)	**Expenses**			*The following is a typical SG&A for some kinds of retail businesses, but your categories and percentages may be different.*
	Staffing costs	104,000	13.0%	The total amount paid to you and your staff as wages and benefits.
	Rent	68,000	8.5%	The total amount paid for store rent. This also includes percentage rent, which is additional rent you pay when sales reach a pre-set amount.
	Utilities	12,800	1.6%	The total amount paid for water, electricity, and heating, ventilation, and air-conditioning (HVAC).
	Maintenance	5,600	0.7%	The total amount paid to fix and maintain items such as equipment and carpeting.
	Telephone and Internet	9,600	1.2%	The total amount paid for telephone service, including long distance, and for an Internet connection.
	Insurance	9,600	1.2%	The total amount paid to insure your business against liability, flood, and fire.
	Supplies	18,400	2.3%	The total amount paid for boxes and bags for customer purchases and store supplies such as letterhead and pens.

Expenses (cont'd)

Advertising	$ 24,000	3.0%	The total amount paid to advertise your business and attract customers to the store, including newspaper, radio, Yellow Pages, and Internet ads, as well as flyers and a company website.
Relationship marketing	6,400	0.8%	The total amount paid for one-to-one communication with your current customers.
Administration	21,600	2.7%	The total amount paid for things such as buying trips and payroll services.
Legal	4,000	0.5%	The total amount paid to your lawyer.
Accounting and data processing	16,000	2.0%	The total amount paid to your accountant for crunching all of the numbers, preparing an annual statement, and filing a tax return.
Technology	16,000	2.0%	The total amount paid for hardware, software, training, and supplies.
Interest expense and statement	4,000	0.5%	The total amount paid as service charges, transaction fees, and interest.
Depreciation	16,000	2.0%	The total amount paid for capital improvements such as fixtures and equipment that you are paying back over time or that is depreciating.
Miscellaneous	4,000	0.5%	The total amount paid for the little things that you could not list anywhere else.
Total expenses	$340,000	42.5%	
(equals) **Net profit**	$ 20,000	2.5%	The total amount you are left with at the end of the year.

SAMPLE 2
THREE PROFIT AND LOSS SCENARIOS

		25% less sales		Original sales		25% more sales	
	Net sales	$600,000	100.0%	$800,000	100.0%	$1,000,000	100.0%
(minus)	Cost of goods sold	$330,000	55.0%	$440,000	55.0%	$550,000	55.0%
(equals)	Gross profit	$270,000	45.0%	$360,000	45.0%	$450,000	45.0%
(minus)	Expenses						
	Staffing costs	84,000	14.0	104,000	13.0	124,000	12.4
	Rent	62,000	10.3	68,000	8.5	74,000	7.4
	Utilities	12,800	2.1	12,800	1.6	12,800	1.3
	Maintenance	5,600	0.9	5,600	0.7	5,600	0.6
	Telephone and Internet	8,800	1.5	9,600	1.2	10,400	1.0
	Insurance	9,600	1.6	9,600	1.2	9,600	1.0
	Supplies	16,800	2.8	18,400	2.3	19,200	1.9
	Advertising and promotion	18,000	3.0	24,000	3.0	30,000	3.0
	Relationship marketing	4,800	0.8	6,400	0.8	8,000	0.8
	Administration	18,000	3.0	21,600	2.7	25,200	2.5
	Legal	4,000	0.7	4,000	0.5	4,000	0.4
	Accounting and data processing	14,000	2.3	16,000	2.0	18,000	1.8
	Technology	16,000	2.7	16,000	2.0	16,000	1.6
	Interest and banking expenses	3,600	0.6	4,000	0.5	4,400	0.4
	Depreciation	16,000	2.7	16,000	2.0	16,000	1.6
	Miscellaneous	3,200	0.5	4,000	0.5	4,800	0.5
	Total expenses	$297,200	49.5%	$340,000	42.5%	$382,000	38.3%
(equals)	Net profit/loss	($27,200)	(4.5%)	$20,000	2.5%	$68,000	6.7%

Third, the secret to running a profitable retail business lies in controlling your expenses. A significant difference between the retail business today and the retail business 35 years ago is that it was much easier for retailers to increase their gross profits back then. When they received new merchandise, they simply attached a higher price to it and customers paid whatever they asked. When there was little competition, that method worked.

Today, however, there is a lot of competition, and customers are extremely price-sensitive. Approximately one in four people shop based on price alone. A favorite question is, "When is this going on sale?" Customers can now check prices on the Internet using only their cell phones — you just can't increase your prices at random in an attempt to increase your gross profit.

Neither will you be able to significantly reduce your cost of goods sold. As an owner-operated retailer, it is unlikely that you will have the upper hand in negotiations with your suppliers or be able to drive prices down by buying larger quantities.

These modern-day realities of the retail business severely restrict your ability to increase your gross profit, and if you cannot increase your gross profit, the only way you can increase your net profit is by reducing your expenses.

The good news is that every dollar you can save in expenses increases your net profit directly. In comparison, it would take additional sales of $40 to add a full dollar to the bottom line in our $800,000 scenario because net profit is just 2.5 percent of the sales figure.

By being price-sensitive, customers are saying that retailers need to be more efficient. In running your business, you will not pay someone to clean the windows or vacuum the floors if they take twice as long as you would to do the same tasks. You simply will not pay for it.

Your customers will not pay you to be inefficient either. They will not pay for a buying trip during which you buy all sorts of ugly merchandise nor for your inability to run a business properly.

a word to the wise

Preparing a pro forma profit and loss statement

At some point while thinking through your business, you will need to take a deep breath and start to prepare a *pro forma* profit and loss statement. This is a profit and loss statement that you prepare in advance of opening your business to determine whether you have a viable business idea. It will also help you describe and define the shape of your business.

Preparing a pro forma profit and loss statement will take literally hundreds of hours of research and planning, and will require you to make a huge number of estimates. While you should be as realistic as possible about all of your estimates, the most important one will be the very first line: your sales plan, or net sales. We strongly suggest that you be conservative in deciding this number because all of your decisions about expenses will flow from it.

To come up with your sales plan estimate, you may find it helpful to answer these three questions:

- What will be the average sale in your store?
- How many customers will you sell to in a day?

  You can visit similar stores to get an idea of how many customers they serve in a day. You may want to increase or decrease the numbers to adjust for size of store and time of year.

- How many days will your store be open in a year?

  You need to allow for the holidays on which stores typically close in your area.

Now let's look at an example. Assume that the average sale in your store will be $44.50, that you will sell to 50 customers a day, and that your store will be open 360 days a year.

What will be the average sale in your store?	(1)	$44.50
How many customers will you sell to in a day?	(2)	50
What amount of business will you do in a day?		
Multiply the average sale in your store (1) by the number of customers you will sell to in a day (2).	(3)	$2,225.00
How many days will your store be open in a year?	(4)	360
What amount of business will you do in a year?		
Multiply the amount of business you will do in a day (3) by the number of days your store will be open in a year (4).	(5)	$801,000.00

You can see the importance of accurate estimates. If the average price of items in your store turns out to be $38.50 instead of $44.50, your sales plan will be off by $108,000 over the year, yet you will have built all of your expense budgets on the higher number.

What will be the average sale in your store?   (1) _____

How many customers will you sell to in a day?   (2) _____

What amount of business will you do in a day?

Multiply the average sale in your store (1) by the number of customers you will sell to in a day (2).   (3) _____

How many days will your store be open in a year?   (4) _____

What amount of business will you do in a year?

Multiply the amount of business you will do in a day (3) by the number of days your store will be open in a year (4).   (5) _____

do the calculation

(We have also included this "volume calculator" as an Excel spreadsheet on the CD-ROM that came with this book.)

Once you are comfortable with your sales plan, you are ready for the second line on your pro forma profit and loss statement and your second most important estimate: your cost of goods sold. To estimate this number, you will need to do some careful research into how much the items you are planning to sell in your store will cost you.

Under the retail method of accounting (see detailed discussion in Chapter 2), retailers express everything as a percentage of the selling price. For example, if you buy an item from your supplier at $24.48 and sell it to your customer at $44.50, your cost of goods sold is 55 percent.

$$\text{Cost of goods sold} = \frac{\text{Price at which you buy}}{\text{Price at which you sell}} = \frac{\$24.48}{\$44.50} = 55\%$$

You will, of course, have many items from many suppliers at many prices in your store. This means that your cost of goods sold will not be an easy number to estimate. You need to start with something, however, so that you can calculate your gross profit.

Then, over a period of perhaps several months, you will need to do some careful research into each of the expense categories on your pro forma profit and loss statement, and estimate the amount you will pay in each category during your first year of operation. This book is designed to help you with the retail-specific items: staffing costs, rent, advertising and promotion, technology, and relationship marketing.

Although the process will be slow, each estimate you make will bring you one step closer to the net profit line and to knowing if you can start and run a profitable retail business, at least on paper. A blank pro forma profit and loss statement is available as an Excel spreadsheet on the CD-ROM.

a word to the wise

Broadly speaking there are two types of people: the creative and the practical. These two groups view the world from very different perspectives. In the retail world, the creative people are the merchants. They tend to have a gut-level love and appreciation for merchandise and the best ways to present it. The practical people are the bean counters. They tend to have a gut-level love and appreciation of numbers and the unshakable truths these numbers represent.

Neither a merchant nor a bean counter can run a successful retail business alone these days. As an owner-operated retailer, you will need to view the world from both perspectives. If you are a creative person, you will need to become somewhat of a bean counter. If you are a practical person, you will need to become somewhat of a merchant.

Adding Value to the Products You Sell by Adopting a Best-Service Strategy

As you think through your store, you will need to make some decisions about your fundamental strategy. You must decide where your retail business will fit into the broad spectrum of retail options. In other words, you will need to decide what you are trying to achieve.

We can help you with many of these decisions by asking one critical question: "Why should a customer shop in your store?" The question is so deceptively simple that the eventual complexity of your answer may surprise you. In part, this answer will come from the way that you add value to the products that manufacturers create.

To be successful, we believe that every retail business needs to add value to its products by adopting one of three basic strategies: offering the greatest assortment, offering the lowest price, or offering the best service. Although these strategies all add value, each one meets the needs of different customers. The challenge you face in retail is to be competitive in all three areas and to clearly exceed your customers' expectations in one of them. Figure 1 summarizes the characteristics of each strategy.

FIGURE 1
ADDED-VALUE STRATEGIES

	Greatest assortment	Lowest price	Best service
Clearly exceeds customers' expectations by providing the added value of:	• an exceptional range or breadth and novelty of product assortments • a uniquely edited selection of products related to a specific lifestyle • a combination of wide assortments within a lifestyle	• price savings and an efficient shopping experience	• customer intimacy based on personalized relationships and individual responsiveness that saves customers shopping time and anxiety • specialized products to meet the needs of individual customers
Devotion to:	• product differentiation	• operational efficiency • elimination of operational waste and costs	• anticipating and solving customer problems • taking responsibility for results • focusing on only those customers who place a premium on this type of service
Characteristics:	• creative selections • special assortments • leading-edge products	• best price • no-hassle shopping	• customized • responsive • personal relationships
Customers say:	• "Their assortment is awesome. If they don't have it, no other store will."	• "You just can't beat their prices. They are the absolute lowest, every day."	• "After we bought it, the sales associate called to see if it was working to our satisfaction."

The greatest assortment strategy involves dominating a product such as toys, office supplies, or furniture. The lowest price strategy involves economies of scale and driving every possible cost out of the business. To adopt either of these two strategies, a retailer must be among the largest in the country, able to purchase in huge quantities and introduce efficiencies that the vast majority of retailers can only dream about.

In today's retail world, the big-box retailers "own" these two strategies. You would need a megastore of 100,000 square feet and millions of dollars worth of inventory just to play in their league.

With the assortment and price strategies taken, the only option left for you is the best-service strategy. Although this strategy comes to you by default, it can be very successful and profitable. Indeed, we believe that the best-service strategy is the very future of owner-operated retail in North America — if you are prepared to walk the walk and make service the heart and soul of your business.

It is easy to answer the question, "Why should a customer shop in my store?" with great-sounding words, but, as anyone who has ever tried to deliver good service knows, the talk is much easier than the walk. To start, you need to structure your business so that everything you do — every strategy, merchandising, buying, human resources, sales management, technology, customer service, and in-store experience decision you make — is focused clearly on service.

That does not mean you can ignore assortment and price as you start to develop a strategic framework for your business. On the contrary, you cannot provide great service if you do not have what your customers want. Neither can you satisfy your customers if your prices are 30 percent higher than the prices at your competitors' stores.

You will need to think carefully about your range of merchandise. As the buyer for your business, you can, in theory, buy anything you want. In reality, you are simply a selector of merchandise for your customers, which means that you really need to understand who your customers are. Once you do, the assortment of merchandise you need to carry in your store will become clear. It will have a focus that comes from your customers.

You will also need to think carefully about your pricing policies. You cannot ignore the fact that customers know and understand the retail marketplace. The same people who shop in your store will see your competitors' advertisements, visit other stores (even in other cities), browse and shop on the Internet, and have a good sense of how much items should cost.

Most of all, you will need to think carefully about your level of service. Eventually, you will find yourself having to decide how many people to schedule for what could be a slow day. Will you decide based on the cost of staffing your store that day or on the level of service you have promised your customers you will deliver *every* day? In other words, how much of your business promise will be just talk and how much of it will be actual and honest walk?

a word to the wise

As consultants, we often see owner-operated retailers trying to follow a strategy of being good at everything. This approach does not work well today. Too many smart and aggressive retailers are finding success offering customers shopping alternatives that are distinctly superior in one important aspect of the business — assortment, price, or service — while being competitive in the other two.

Adopting a specific marketing and operational strategy gives these stores a competitive advantage that adds value to the products they sell and makes them stand out as superior to the competition.

Focusing or not focusing resources in a single direction is why some stores succeed while others fail. The successful stores know where they are going and how to get there. The others usually lack a viable, strategic plan to achieve their goals and wind up being mediocre at everything. This means that they fail to distinguish themselves in their customers' eyes and fail to meet their customers' needs.

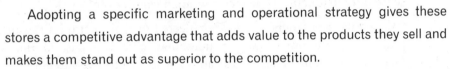

Developing a Strategic Framework

Once you have thought carefully about assortment, price, and service, you need to go one step farther in developing the strategic framework for your business. You need to come up with your *secret weapon*: the one thing that your store can provide that no other store can deliver. This is important regardless of what products you sell. If you do not have a secret weapon, your business will be just the same as every other owner-operated retail business that sells similar products and competes in the service arena. Customers will have no compelling reason to shop in your store.

Developing your secret weapon

You should choose your secret weapon based on the needs of your customers. To do this you need to keep a basic marketing lesson in mind: customers do not need to buy drills, they need to buy holes. In other words, there is always a deeper level or purpose to their apparent needs.

If you ran an eyewear store, your secret weapon might be that you are an artisan who can produce custom-made eyewear. Instead of just talking about glasses, you might talk about "unique, handcrafted frames that complement a unique personality." This statement appeals to both the apparent need, which is glasses, and to a deeper need, which is individuality. Your store could adopt this custom-made aspect as the secret weapon it will seek to deliver effectively.

The big question then is whether there are enough customers who need both glasses and individuality for your eyewear store to be successful. More to the point, are there enough customers who need your product and the sense of individuality your secret weapon can deliver?

Because customers' needs are reflected in their attitudes toward shopping, understanding these attitudes may give you part of the answer. Generally, customers' attitudes can be divided into five categories.

Quality shoppers put quality and fashion before price. They enjoy shopping and prefer a moderate degree of personal service. Moderately loyal to a few stores, they tend not to like mass merchandisers. These customers are typically well educated, hold prestigious jobs, and have high incomes. They make up about 10 percent of the market.

Intensely store loyal, *specialty shoppers* typically shop at specialty stores and traditional department stores. Price is far less important to them than quality, fashion, and in-store service. Mainly older, affluent couples with good jobs and incomes, these customers tend to dislike shopping. They make up about 15 percent of the market.

Sociable shoppers want and expect personal in-store service. They remain loyal to a few stores, especially the traditional department stores, for most personal items and furniture. Many are older or retired, with ample time to shop. These customers avoid mass merchandisers, except for toys and domestics. They make up about 10 percent of the market.

Primarily young and middle-aged families with moderate incomes and two or more children, *price-sensitive nonshoppers* rely on discounters and mass merchandisers except for items such as fashion. They do not especially like shopping around, but are forced into it by their moderate incomes. Price-sensitive nonshoppers often have difficulty finding time to shop and consider in-store service a low priority. They make up about 35 percent of the market.

Price-sensitive shoppers are also price-sensitive, but they like to shop. Requiring little in-store service, they do not adopt new fashions early and they are not especially loyal to stores. Most of them have young families and rely on mass merchandisers for nearly all of the items they buy. With lower levels of education and downscale jobs and incomes, they make up about 30 percent of the market.

Keeping these very different attitudes in mind — and the apparent and deeper needs that each one implies — you need to think carefully about five critical questions as you complete the strategic framework for your business. Your ultimate success or failure could well depend on your finding good answers to these questions:

1. Why should a customer shop in your store? _____

_____

_____

2. What is the role of price competitiveness in your store? _____

_____

_____

3. What is the level of merchandise assortment in your store? _____

_____

_____

4. What is the level of service in your store? _____

_____

_____

5. What is your secret weapon? _____

_____

_____

(This is available as a worksheet entitled Developing Your Secret Weapon on the CD-ROM.)

a word to the wise

The following is not a complete strategic framework for an owner-operated retail business because it does not include the store's secret weapon, but it is a good start:

"My store will be competitive in price with other stores in the market, but I will not meet discount-store prices. I will shop my competitors regularly and make sure that I am never more than 20 percent higher than the lowest price in the market.

"I will carry an assortment that is important to my customers and never be out of stock on basic items, but I will not dominate any merchandise classification.

"I will earn my margins and truly amaze my customers by providing the best service they can find, service that goes the extra mile. This will include detailed product knowledge, a pleasant atmosphere, after-sale service, free delivery, and a make-it-right returns policy."

Developing a Clear Vision of Your Business

Although you have no real alternative but to build your business around service, you have almost total freedom after that to create any kind of business that you can picture in your mind. Because the business will be a reflection of who you are, this vision must come from you. It is not something that anyone else can provide for you.

This book can, however, help you develop a clear vision. The best way to do this is to pretend that you are your store's first customer on opening day. You are standing outside a retail business that you have never seen before, and you will decide in mere seconds whether or not it is worth entering the store. Through the eyes of your customer, what does that store look like? What is it like once you enter? Use Worksheet 1, Developing a Clear Vision, to jot down what you see. (This is also included on the CD-ROM.)

This exercise of picturing your business in your mind is every bit as important as developing a pro forma profit and loss statement. It will be a process rather than an event — a process in which you literally close your eyes and spend hours seeing, hearing, touching, tasting, and smelling the business you are about to create. Your vision describes the merchant half of

WORKSHEET 1
DEVELOPING A CLEAR VISION

Exterior and exterior sign:_____

_____

Window displays:_____

_____

New experience or "same old":_____

_____

General atmosphere:_____

_____

Overall visual appeal:_____

_____

General organization:_____

_____

Color and texture:_____

_____

Mood set by lighting:_____

_____

Everything visible from the front door:_____

_____

Spotlights highlight merchandise:_____

_____

Front-and-forward displays:_____

_____

Displays with props, related merchandise:_____

_____

Brand names evident:_____

_____

Merchandise in departments:_____

_____

Presentation tells a story:_____

_____

Printed product information:_____

_____

Price tickets and signs:_____

_____

Consistency of interior signs:_____

_____

Sign holders:_____

_____

Number of sales associates:_____

Staff appearance and identification:_____

Level of in-store service:_____

Level of product knowledge:_____

Type of shopping experience:_____

Price range:_____

Price competitiveness:_____

Value:_____

Merchandise quality:_____

Merchandise "romance":_____

Special sales:_____

Speed at checkout:_____

Payment methods:_____

Delivery service:_____

Returns policy:_____

Music:_____

Neat and clean:_____

Other:_____

Other:_____

Other:_____

your business. It will take as much work and effort as describing the bean counter half of your business through your pro forma profit and loss statement.

Identifying and Studying Your Three Most Important Direct Competitors

Without limiting the creative process, you will clearly have to stay in contact with the real world as you develop your vision. To start and run a profitable retail business, you will need to find a niche somewhere in today's competitive retail marketplace. You need to find some aspect of your target customers' needs that your competition is not meeting or identify some subgroup of your target customers who have needs that your competition is not meeting.

You should visit those stores that you perceive to be direct competitors while you are developing your vision. These are stores in the same business and which are serving the same customers as you, which means that you must take business away from them in order to grow profitably.

You can tell if a store is a direct competitor by answering one question: "If customers do not buy a given item from my store, will they be able to buy it from the other store instead?" If the answer is yes, the other store is a direct competitor.

If your store is quite different or even unique, you may not have direct competitors. In this case, you should visit those stores that you perceive as *indirect* competitors. These are stores in a different business but serving the same customers as you, which means that you *may* have to take business away from them in order to grow profitably.

In addition to visiting the stores that you perceive to be direct or indirect competitors, you should also visit those stores that your customers perceive to be alternatives to your business. You may need to speak with some of your target customers to get this information, but it will be worth the effort.

For example, we mentioned earlier that specialty shoppers typically shop at specialty stores and traditional department stores. If your target customers are specialty shoppers, department stores could well be your main competition. It is obviously better to know this when you are designing your business than to discover it when your business is already open and you have fewer ways of making changes.

By visiting what you perceive to be your direct or indirect competitors and examining what your customers perceive to be the alternatives to shopping in your store, you will develop a good understanding of the diversity that exists in the retail marketplace today. You will also come back with a lot of ideas that will help clarify your vision of your business.

After you examine all of the competition in a general way, you should identify your three most important competitors and examine those businesses in more detail. By knowing their strengths and weaknesses, you will be able to design your business in a way that avoids their strengths and either attacks or simply fills in around their weaknesses.

The same categories you used to develop a clear vision for your business will also help you analyze your three most important competitors. Use Worksheet 2, Analyzing Your Competitors. Remember how important it is to look at a store through the eyes of a customer; at the same time, look for things that a customer would only perceive subconsciously.

that's a good idea

While developing your vision, you may want to take a working holiday and visit some of the best retailers in cities such as Chicago, Los Angeles, Montreal, New York, San Francisco, Seattle, Toronto, and Vancouver. This is the logical next step to take after looking at your three most important competitors, and it is a great investment in your future.

You do not need to know in advance which retailers are considered the best — they will jump out at you as you browse the malls and walk through the shopping districts. The idea is not to copy another retailer but to experience firsthand what makes the best retailers stand out from the rest. Spending one or two hours in each store will open your eyes to specific aspects of the competition that customers see every day. Be sure to take along extra printouts of the Analyzing Your Competitors worksheet to take extensive notes about each store you visit.

After you have fully developed your strategy, you will need to start thinking about how you can convey your strategic message to customers through various kinds of communication. We use the word *communication* as an umbrella term to describe all of the ways that you give customers information about your business through sights, sound, written communication, signals, or behavior. This section covers the three most important forms of communication: store location, store design and layout, and advertising.

WORKSHEET 2
ANALYZING YOUR COMPETITORS

	Competitor: _____ Date visited: _____	Competitor: _____ Date visited: _____	Competitor: _____ Date visited: _____
Exterior and exterior sign			
Window displays			
New experience or "same old"			
General atmosphere			
Overall visual appeal			
General organization			
Color and texture			
Mood set by lighting			
Everything visible from the front door			
Spotlights highlight merchandise			
Front-and-forward displays			
Displays with props, related merchandise			
Brand names evident			
Merchandise in departments			
Presentation tells a story			

WORKSHEET 2 — Continued

	Competitor: _____ Date visited: _____	Competitor: _____ Date visited: _____	Competitor: _____ Date visited: _____
Printed product information			
Price tickets and signs			
Consistency of interior signs			
Sign holders			
Number of sales associates			
Staff appearance and identification			
Level of in-store service			
Level of product knowledge			
Type of shopping experience			
Price range			
Price competitiveness			
Value			
Merchandise quality			
Merchandise "romance"			
Special sales			
Speed at checkout			

	Competitor: _____ Date visited: _____	Competitor: _____ Date visited: _____	Competitor: _____ Date visited: _____
Payment methods			
Delivery service			
Returns policy			
Music			
Neat and clean			
Other: _____			
Other: _____			
Other: _____			

Conveying Your Strategic Message Through Your Store Location

The most important communication you have with customers is your store location. A time-honored cliché says that the three most important factors to consider when opening a retail business are location, location, and location. Figure 2 outlines the strengths and weaknesses of the various location types that you may want to consider for your business.

FIGURE 2
STORE LOCATION CONSIDERATIONS

Location	Strengths	Weaknesses
Downtown	• central • big draw • office market • a lot of service and culture	• parking problems • distance from suburbs • quality of location varies
Regional shopping center	• drawing power • good parking and access • mass market	• distance may be too great for convenience merchandise • high cost base
Community shopping center	• close to market • good parking • good traffic from food stores	• may not specialize • can be hurt by downtown and regional centers
Strip malls or street locations	• convenience • low cost base • can specialize	• local traffic only • small geographic base of shoppers • transit, parking problems
Warehouse or industrial district	• low cost base • budget image	• location not typical for shopping — low traffic • requires heavy promotion

With good reason, many owner-operated retailers are concerned about the seemingly high rent charged in shopping centers. However, to really understand which location is right for your business, you will need to evaluate all the options in terms of *value*. In other words, you should not look just at occupancy costs or arbitrarily decide that any given rent is too high. You will be paying for customer traffic in one way or another. If you pay less in rent, you will have to pay more in advertising and promotion. If you pay more in rent, you will have to pay less in advertising and promotion.

If you locate on a street, you will probably pay less in rent, but you will have relatively fewer stores nearby to help you generate customer traffic. Because of this, you will have to allocate more money to advertising and promotion.

In a shopping center, the synergy created by many stores being together in one facility tends to increase the number of customers who walk by your door, and the center's relatively large advertising budget can increase traffic even more. You will pay for this traffic through the higher rent that shopping centers charge, but you will be able to allocate less money for advertising and promotion.

Sample 3 shows how one retailer compared two different locations. The total costs of location B are more than double the total costs of location A — and yet the cost per shopper is less than half. In terms of value, location B is the better choice. (Use the Location Calculator worksheet to compare two locations on your own. We have included this as an Excel spreadsheet on the CD-ROM.)

a word to the wise

> Negotiating and signing a retail lease is not something that you should do alone. Negotiating is a complex process, and the actual document you sign contains page after page of terms and conditions that have very precise legal meanings. Because you are a retailer and not a lease negotiator or a lawyer, we strongly suggest that you get professional guidance and advice.

SAMPLE 3
COMPARING THE VALUE OF LOCATIONS

	Location A $ per square foot	Location B $ per square foot
Occupancy costs		
Fixed rent	$ 80	$200
Overhead	10	40
Common area costs	20	30
Total occupancy costs	$110	$270
Advertising and promotion costs		
Advertising	$20	$40
Display and sales promotion	20	40
Total advertising and promotion costs	$40	$80
Total costs	$150	$350
Customer traffic per week	20,000	100,000
Cost per shopper	$ 0.0075	$ 0.0035

Conveying Your Strategic Message Through Your Store Design and Layout

The second most important communication you have with customers is through your store design and layout. We will look at these from a retailer's perspective here and revisit them when we look at things from a customer's perspective in Chapter 8.

Store design and layout are the first things that customers see as they browse through the mall or walk down the street, so these need to be in complete harmony with your strategic framework. If they are not, you will have wasted much of the time you spent developing a vision of your business.

We recall one owner-operated retailer who sought professional guidance because her sales were not meeting her plan. This retailer was a talented young fashion designer in a medium-size city. She had built a beautiful store with columns on the façade flanking elegant display windows. The look was expensive and top of the line. On the inside, however, her prices were quite reasonable considering the high-quality designer merchandise she carried.

This retailer needed to unscramble the mixed message that she was giving to customers. The solution was to place tasteful price tags on the items in the display windows. Customers who had previously assumed that one of this designer's creations would cost $500, and had not entered the store for that reason, learned to their surprise that the price was only half that amount.

As this retailer's communication became clearer, both customer traffic and sales moved closer to plan.

One of the important factors determining whether customers will return to your store is how enjoyable and efficient they find the shopping experience. This begins with layout. Your store design should make it easy for customers to get in, get around, and get out. For this to happen, you will need to have logical aisle patterns and locations for each merchandise, service, and support area.

The Developing a Clear Vision worksheet discussed earlier touches on some of the most important aspects of store design and layout, but you should pay particular attention to the following factors:

- The exterior should be inviting, with display windows that indicate to customers what your store is all about. These can be formal, with closed backs, or informal, with open backs. The total exterior should be interesting and eye-catching, and should convey the strategic framework of the business.

- You should change your window displays often so customers do not start to view your business as a museum instead of a store. Windows send a clear message to your customers, and that message is every bit as important as any newspaper ad. Because you are a professional retailer and not a professional display artist, you should retain someone for this job on a contract basis.

- Your outside signage is another critical part of what you are saying to your customer. If you are a trendy fashion retailer, you will need to have a trendy sign, and it should look very different from the sign above the nearby pet store.

- The prime real estate in your store is within the 20-foot semicircle just inside the front door. This will clearly be the most productive merchandising area in your store, since all of your customers will walk through it, but don't put anything too important within the first 10 feet because many customers won't even notice it. To welcome customers into this area, your entrance should always be open and inviting.

- In-store displays can really help customers understand your store and its merchandise. They let people see a product without packaging and in context with related items. Sometimes referred to as silent salespeople, good in-store displays can dramatically increase your sales. However, they can also convey a messy image if you do not tidy and reorganize them regularly.

- Your in-store signage is critically important, although sometimes you will wonder if customers actually read it. Handwritten signs reflect poorly on your business and, given the wide availability of instant printing shops and desktop publishing programs, we can see no reason to use them. The design of your signs should be consistent throughout the store and be changed often enough to keep the look of the store fresh.

- Any in-store posters must also fit your message. Although vendor-supplied advertising may be attractive and cheap, it may not be appropriate. You may be better off throwing it away or going back to your vendor to request something that does fit your message.

- Your walls are extremely powerful merchandising areas because you can display products vertically to a greater height than you can in the center of the store. Because sales per square foot are always greatest along the walls, store planners often build central interior walls to give a store additional wall space.

- The width of the aisles in your store should reflect both the scale of the store and your customer traffic, but they should never be less than 4 feet wide and never more than 12 feet wide. Fixtures in the center of the store should not exceed 5 feet in height; 4 feet would be better.

- The ceiling height of a store should generally be somewhere between 14 and 18 feet. Whatever it is, it should be unobtrusive. You will want to draw your customers' eyes to the merchandise, not to the ceiling. Dark colors tend to make a ceiling seem lower, while light colors tend to increase the visual height.

- Fluorescent lights are great for economy but incandescent lights are by far the best for lighting merchandise. Track lighting will let you aim spotlights and floodlights at important display areas. Many stores now use low-voltage lighting systems that are expensive but very effective.

- Floor treatments should be easy to maintain, but they should also respect the needs of sales associates who will be standing all day. Tile is easy to maintain but hard to stand on. Carpet is harder to maintain but easier to stand on. Often, a mix of surfaces can accommodate the needs of both the business and its employees.

a word to the wise

Whether you are starting from scratch or planning to renovate an existing store, you should work with an experienced designer.

To begin the process, you should visit stores you like and ask who did the design. You should then contact those designers, plus one or two others, and outline your vision of your business. You should explain clearly that your basic strategy is service and ask how design can support that strategy.

By the time you speak with a designer, you should have a good understanding of what departments need to go where in your store and the budget that you have to spend.

A good designer will talk to you in terms of sales productivity and not just elegant design. His or her role should be to add ideas, creativity, and experience to your strategy and vision. You should judge the designer's suitability based on the way he or she can support your service strategy, relate to your target market, create a unique image, and effectively display merchandise while supporting the service component of your business.

Conveying Your Strategic Message Through Your Advertising

The third most important communication you have with customers is your advertising. This will be especially important during your first year of operation when you need to spread the word and tell your target customers about your secret weapon — the way that your business alone can meet both their apparent and their deeper needs.

By the end of your first year of operation, you will have served thousands of customers, identified your best customers, and developed a relationship-marketing program — a process we will describe in Chapter 7. At that point, you will want to set aside some of your advertising and promotion budget for relationship marketing. Until then, the full amount should go to advertising.

You can use a wide range of media to advertise your new business. Figure 3 shows the reach, cost, and market for each. In this table —

- *reach* refers to the number of people you are speaking to at once,
- *cost* refers to how expensive it is to advertise using this medium compared to others, and
- *market* refers to the extent to which you can target or focus your message.

FIGURE 3
ADVERTISING OPTIONS

Medium	Reach	Cost	Market
Catalogs	Individual	Moderate/high	Personal/mass
Coupons	Broad	Low	Mass
Direct mail*	Individual	Low	Personal
Display	Local	Low	In-store
Flyers*	Local	Low	Custom
Internet*	Exceptionally broad	Moderate	Mass or special interest
Local cable TV	Broad	Moderate	Mass
Local TV	Broad	High	Mass
Magazines	Broad	Moderate/high	Mass
Newspapers*	Broad	Moderate	Mass
Outdoor	Broad	Moderate	Mass
Radio	Broad	Moderate	Mass
Signage (in-store)	Local	Low	In-store
Word of mouth*	Individual	Low	Personal
Yellow Pages*	Broad	Moderate	Mass

*Most important for owner-operated retailers

As an illustration of how this table works, consider newspaper advertising:

- The reach is broad because many people buy the paper. Depending on the newspaper, you may be able to reach potential customers anywhere in your community, city, region, or country.

- The cost of newspaper advertising is usually moderate, depending on the size of ad you run and the rates charged by the paper.

- The market for newspaper advertising is mass market. You do not know who will read your ad: a multimillionaire flying on a private jet or someone using the paper to shield his or her eyes from the sun while sleeping on a park bench.

Flyers, by comparison, have a local reach. You can often work with a flyer-distribution company or the post office to target a very specific neighborhood or area. For example, you might choose an area in which you have fewer customers than you think you should have. The cost of flyers can be very low if you focus on a particular area.

The Yellow Pages can be a powerful form of advertising for attracting new customers to your store. Many people *do* let their fingers do the walking. The difficulty with Yellow Pages advertising is that you need to book your space far in advance and design an ad that can last a full year. Your Yellow Pages message should be concise and easy to understand because potential customers literally just flip through the pages.

At a time when many individuals have their own website, it seems obvious that businesses should have them, too. After all, customers will be able to find and contact you from anywhere in the world. But ask yourself: Is that really what I hope to achieve? In the final analysis, for most owner-operated retailers, the Internet is just another type of advertising. If you decide to have a website, remember that the advertising you deliver through your website should match the look and feel of all your other advertising, and if you decide to sell products online, your customer service should match the high-quality service you provide in your store.

Truly, the most important advertising medium for any owner-operated retailer is direct mail. The reach is individual, letting you shoot right at the target, the cost is low, and the market is very personal. During your first year of operation, you may want to purchase a commercial mailing list to augment the one you are building.

Word-of-mouth advertising is the most powerful advertising category on the list. Its reach is individual, its cost is incredibly low, and it works at the same personal level as direct mail. We will talk later about the critical importance of providing extra-mile service so that you can create, encourage, and build on the power of word-of-mouth advertising.

that's a good idea

As you make your plans, you may want to know the percentage of advertising dollars retailers typically spend on each option.

Direct mail..35%

Relationship marketing.....................15%

Newspapers..10%

Website 10%

Radio 10%

Other 9.5%
(Includes catalogs, coupons, flyers, local cable TV, local TV, magazines, outdoor billboards, Yellow Pages)

Display 5.5%

Signage (in-store)...............................5%

Note that newspaper advertising has been steadily declining for some time now and is being replaced with direct mail, Internet, and relationship marketing.

Your Advertising Plan

All advertising costs money and to manage this expenditure, you will need to develop an advertising plan similar to the one shown in Sample 4. (A blank copy of this form is also included on the CD-ROM.) In developing this plan, we suggest that you follow the slogan: Fish while the fish are biting. By this we mean that the money you spend on advertising in a given period should be directly proportional to the business you expect to do in that period. If your objective is to push sales 10 percent higher, it makes sense to strive for a 10 percent increase in sales during a peak-sales month rather than a slow month.

For example, if December is your peak month, you should put much of your advertising money into late November and early December. We suggest starting in late November because when you are planning promotional advertising (as opposed to clearance advertising), you should always launch the campaign ahead of the selling period.

ADVERTISING PLAN
(FOR YEAR TWO, INCLUDES RELATIONSHIP MARKETING)

	Clearance		Spring			Summer			Fall		Christmas		Total
	Jan.	Feb.	March	April	May	June	July	Aug.	Sept.	Oct.	Nov.	Dec.	
Sales last year	$35,000	$30,000	$60,000	$58,000	$65,000	$62,000	$45,000	$45,000	$62,000	$70,000	$78,000	$150,000	$760,000
Sales plan	$40,000	$32,000	$64,000	$60,000	$68,000	$64,000	$48,000	$48,000	$64,000	$72,000	$80,000	$160,000	$800,000
Catalogs													$0
Coupons													$0
Direct mail			$1,500	$1,000	$1,000	$1,000		$1,000	$2,000	$2,000	$2,000		$11,500
Display			$200	$150	$200	$200		$250	$150	$150	$300	$150	$1,750
Flyers									$1,000		$1,000		$2,000
Internet	$300	$300	$300	$300	$300	$300	$300	$300	$300	$300	$300	$300	$3,600
Local TV													$0
Relationship marketing	$400	$400	$400	$400	$400	$400	$400	$400	$400	$400	$400	$400	$4,800
Magazines													$0
Newspapers	$300		$300			$300		$600		$600	$500	$500	3,400
Outdoor													$0
Radio								$800	$900		$900	$1,000	$3,600
Signage	$250		$200		$250		$200		$250		$250		$1,400
Word of mouth	FREE	FREE	FREE	FREE	FREE	FREE	FREE	FREE	FREE	FREE	FREE	FREE	$0
Yellow Pages	$200	$200	$200	$200	$200	$200	$200	$200	$200	$200	$200	$200	$2,400
Total	$1,450	$900	$3,100	$2,050	$2,650	$2,400	$1,100	$3,550	$5,200	$3,650	$5,850	$2,550	$34,450
% to sales plan	3.63%	2.81%	4.84%	3.42%	3.90%	3.75%	2.29%	7.40%	8.13%	5.07%	7.31%	1.59%	4.31%

The other thing to consider when developing an advertising plan is that you must cover your breakeven expenses each month regardless of the sales volume you achieve. If you allow a certain amount for "maintenance" advertising each month, it can help generate sales to cover these costs.

When planning their advertising, many retailers split the year into five periods. The unique sales pattern of your business may lead you to use fewer time periods than the five we show on our sample plan or give less emphasis to the Christmas selling season.

Developing an advertising plan will help you look at advertising the same way you look at every other expenditure — as a percentage of sales. That is why you start by entering onto your advertising plan your expected sales from your sales plan and then divide it up into months. You then work line by line through the various options, planning this much for newspaper during your January clearance, that much for a flyer to announce your spring season, and so on.

We have no fixed rule for how much you should budget for advertising. However, the absolute maximum for an owner-operated retailer is 5 percent of sales; the absolute minimum is 2 percent of sales. Somewhere in between is probably right for you.

that's a good idea

You should plan your promotions carefully so that you avoid black holes of inactivity. You can do this by using a combination of weekly and monthly promotional events.

Weekly promotional events are effective because they help you create a sense of urgency for customers to shop *now* for that week's featured specials. Any occasion for gift-giving represents a great opportunity to use a weekly theme to link your store with your customers' need to purchase a gift — for example, a Valentine's Day gift in February or a Father's Day gift in June.

Monthly promotional events are umbrellas that reinforce the overall position of your store during the most important times of the retail year — for example, Christmas or back-to-school. These events take advantage of the longer time period to reinforce the store's advertising as the best place to shop by integrating the whole look of your business, including windows, signage, special bags, and employee name badges.

W e suggest that you pause here to look back over the topics we have covered in this chapter on the basics of retail. While everything is fresh in your mind, you need to decide how well prepared you are for this part of an owner-operated retailer's job.

You then need to decide what three issues on the basics of retail you can work on immediately, what three pieces of additional information you need, and which three people you should telephone or meet with soon.

How well prepared are you for the basics of retail? (Circle one.)

READINESS		RATING
Need to hire a consultant	✏	1
Need to take some courses	✏	2
Need to read some books	✏	3
Can handle this with effort	✏	4
Can handle this in my sleep	✏	5

What three basics of retail issues can you work on immediately, and what can you do about each of them?

1_____

2_____

3_____

What three pieces of additional information do you need to better understand the basics of retail?

1_____

2_____

3_____

Which three people should you telephone or meet with soon about the basics of the retail part of your job?

1_____

2_____

3_____

Please transfer these answers to the Action Plan in Appendix 1.

2
MERCHANDISING

This part of your job includes:

- Grouping your merchandise into departments and classifications

- Tracking your customers' votes by tracking all of their purchases

- Learning from your customers what they want to buy from you

- Using the retail method of accounting in your retail business

- Monitoring your business using a monthly maintained margin report

- Bringing control to your business through four key operating ratios

- Using time-limited promotional markdowns to stimulate your sales

- Using regular markdowns to adjust your inventory to market value

- Increasing your credibility by using a seasonal markdown philosophy

your job description

where you want to go

Grouping Merchandise into Departments and Classifications

Grouping the items in your store into *departments* and *classifications* is one of the most important things you can do to ensure the success of your retail business. In fact, it will be almost impossible to run a *profitable* retail business if you do not build a department and classification discipline into it right from the start.

If you had started your business in 1950, you would have run it with little or no structure. Using the latest technology, you would have used an adding machine to total your day's sales and a cash drawer to hold the money. At the end of the day, you would have known that you had made a total of $500 in sales. However, the adding machine tape would not have told you what items you sold to get that $500.

If you had started your business in 1970, the evolution of cash registers would have encouraged you to structure your business a little bit more. You would have used either a manual or an electric cash register to track your sales by department. At the end of the day, you would have known from the cash register tape that you had made a total of $900 in sales and that you had sales of $300 in department one, $400 in department two, and $200 in department three.

A department is a grouping of merchandise that could stand alone as a specialty store. For example, a drugstore could move its cosmetics department to a smaller location, or a department store could move its home furnishings department into the mall. In theory, both could succeed as separate businesses.

As you think through the selection of merchandise you will offer in your store, keep in mind that you should keep the number of departments under control. Each department should account for at least 10 percent of your business. Therefore, the maximum you can have in your store is ten departments. Some successful stores have only one, while most have three or four departments.

Department totals, by themselves, do not provide all that much useful information. You really need to understand at a deeper level what is, and what is not, selling each day — and perhaps even each hour.

The development of personal computers was a real breakthrough that enabled owner-operated retailers to take charge of merchandise management. Anyone who has started a retail business since 1990 has been able to structure it to a very fine level of detail. Use the tracking methods we describe in this chapter, and you will know at the end of the day — or whenever you want the information — that you made a total of $4,500 in sales. And that you had sales of $1,500 in department one, $2,000 in department two and $1,000 in department three. And that you sold, for example, 12 widescreen DVDs and eight full-screen DVDs of a particular movie title. The information you can obtain is endless, and the insights you can gain are amazing.

that's a good idea

We often remind retailers that customers vote with their wallets, meaning that the most valuable market research you will ever have is the behavior of your customers. You could do all kinds of research to ask customers what they would like to buy in your store, but the answers would all be theoretical. The only answers that really count are the ones that customers provide when they put their money on the counter to pay for their purchases.

If you do not count the votes of your customers through their purchases, you will not last long in the retail business. You cannot afford to ignore the crucial information that people will give you every day through their behavior.

Learning from Your Customers What They Want to Buy from You

Although you will learn a great deal about your customers and their preferences if you track your sales by department, you will learn even more if you track sales at a finer level of detail — by categories or classifications within your departments. (Categories and classifications are the same thing. Both words refer to a grouping or assortment of merchandise that customers view as interchangeable.)

Your customers will define the classifications in your store by the way they shop. If you are a hardware retailer and you are sold out of hammers, your customers will not buy a can of paint and use that to pound in nails instead. Hammers and paint are in different product classifications. If you are a women's clothing retailer and you are sold out of dresses, your customers will not buy bathing suits to wear to work instead. Dresses and bathing suits are in different product classifications.

When customers come into your store looking for particular items, their needs can often be met by several items from the same product classification, but never by items from other product classifications. Figure 4 shows how assigning classifications works.

The same rule of thumb applies to a classification as applies to a department: each classification should account for at least 10 percent of the business in that department. Therefore, the maximum you can have in each department is ten classifications.

The actual number you choose will be a trade-off between your need for accurate information and your ability to digest that information in a meaningful way. You may decide that different departments need to have different numbers of classifications. The key is to let your customers be your guide. If you have too many classifications, some will inevitably represent only a small percentage of your total business. In this way, your customers will be telling you that they do not believe yours is the right store at which to buy items in that classification.

To be a successful retailer, you need to recognize that you cannot be everything for everybody. "I am sorry, but I don't carry that item," is one of the hardest things you will ever say to a customer — but you *must* say it to certain customers.

For example, if your business is a shoe store, you may decide that you will not carry shoes for children, not stock athletic shoes, or not stock wider sizes.

Assuming that you have a good POS (point of sale) system (which we will discuss in Chapter 6), it will be much easier to understand this once your store has been open and operating for six months. You will then be able to start tailoring your inventory to the votes you got from customers during the first season. Carrying the items that your customers want to buy is one of the most critical things you can do to become an important source of that merchandise for them.

A big advantage to organizing your business around classifications is that you will discover a lot about your customers. You will learn that they prefer some classifications to others in your store and that they will spend a certain amount of money in each classification. You can buy accordingly and give them more of what they want the following season.

FIGURE 4
CLASSIFYING YOUR MERCHANDISE

Subclassifications are further definitions of a classification. For example, if you are a menswear retailer who does good business in your dress-shirt classification, you might want to have two subclassifications: one called *long-sleeved dress shirts* and another called *short-sleeved dress shirts*.

Within each subclassification, you might want to divide things further into lines, items, and stock keeping units (SKUs) — the finest level of detail at which you can define an item. For example:

Department:	menswear
Classification:	dress shirt
Subclassification:	long-sleeved dress shirt
Line:	Arrow brand long-sleeved dress shirt
Item:	Button-down collar, white, 100% cotton, Arrow brand, long-sleeved dress shirt
SKU:	Size 16½–34, button-down collar, white, 100% cotton, Arrow brand, long-sleeved dress shirt

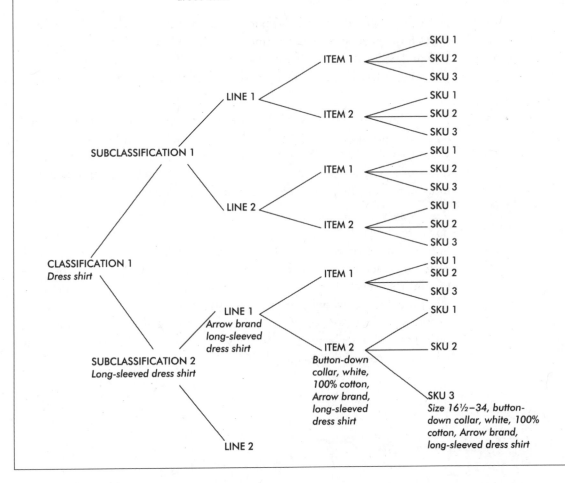

For example, if you are a menswear retailer selling dress shirts, you might learn that 80 percent of the votes in your dress shirt classification went to items priced between $75 and $85. You might also learn that 90 percent of *those* votes went to your long-sleeved dress shirt subclassification, and that 50 percent of *those* votes went to the Arrow brand.

If that was confusing, follow the math:

80% of your total dress-shirt votes went to the $75 to $85 price range.	0.80×1	$= 0.80$
90% of that 80% went to long-sleeved dress shirts (72%).	0.90×0.80	$= 0.72$
50% of that 72% went to the Arrow brand (36%).	0.50×0.72	$= 0.36$

Where should you put 36 percent of your dollars when you buy dress shirts for next season? Arrow brand long-sleeved dress shirts priced between $75 and $85 would be a great place to start. If you had more information, you could carry this analysis right down to the size, style, color, and fabric level.

Without this knowledge, you could easily put 50 percent of your dollars into shirts priced at $100 and then face huge markdowns next season when they do not sell. Worse, you could put 50 percent of your dollars into shirts priced at $60 and face an entire season in which you can match your unit sales from the previous year but not your dollar sales.

Using a computer, you will be able to capture sales information right down to the stock keeping unit (SKU) level. In reality, you will probably find this information too much to comprehend. You will have thousands of SKU sales each week or month, and you will not be able to wrap your head around that level of detail. Even the item, line, and subclassification levels will probably be overwhelming, so we suggest that you just look at classifications. In fact, we believe that you should manage the entire merchandising side of your business at the classification level. We will demonstrate how in the rest of this chapter.

If you take full advantage of technology in your business, it will give you a level of information and control that most owner-operated retailers lack. At the end of every day, you will be able to look at your sales by department to see if you are meeting your goals.

If you are, everything is fine and you can go home to rest.

If you are not meeting your goals, you will be able to "drill down" to the classification level and find out why. Perhaps you will find that within a certain department, classifications one and two are performing well but classification three is nowhere near budget. Once you know that, you can go home with a clear understanding of what you need to look at first when you come in the next morning.

Depending on whether or not you plan to reorder specific products, you may want to extend your level of information and control right down to the individual SKUs within the classification.

that's a good idea

Using the Retail Method of Accounting

Because operating a retail business is very different from operating any other kind of business, both the IRS and the Canada Revenue Agency allow retailers to use a unique method of accounting known as the *retail method*. Also called the *dual book system*, this system acknowledges the fact that as a retailer, you need to use a two-column ledger in order to understand your business fully.

In the left-hand column, you will keep a running record of the cost of your merchandise — the landed price, which is cost plus shipping. In the right-hand column, you will keep a running record of the retail value of that merchandise — the total you would get if you added up the price tickets of all of the items in your store.

Although the retail method of accounting offers significant advantages for a retail business of any size — we will outline just some of them here — many accountants are not familiar with the system and will set up your books using one of the traditional cost methodologies instead. This will rob you of some of the most important information that any retail owner can have, including information that helps you compare operating results with those of other retailers. It is also less expensive than a cost-based system, provides more control, and lets you get financial statements much sooner. Find an accountant who either knows or will learn the retail method of accounting.

Monitoring Your Business Using a Monthly Maintained Margin Report

Under the retail method, the monthly maintained margin report is an important document. It shows you how much profit you made last month and gives you a reality check on the health of your business. You do this report at the classification level.

In the report shown in Sample 5, the beginning inventory is $25,000 at cost for this product classification (see Line 1). This represents $62,000 at selling price.

The most basic formula in retail is cost plus markup equals selling price.

Cost	+	Markup	= Selling price
$25,000	+	$37,000	= $62,000

Under the retail method, the selling price of an item is always 100 percent. Therefore both cost (the amount you pay for an item) and markup (the amount by which you increase the price to cover your expenses and your profit) can be expressed as a percentage of the selling price.

Cost	+	Markup	= Selling price
$25,000	+	$37,000	= $62,000
40.3%	+	59.7%	= 100%

Neither cost nor markup can ever be more than 100 percent. For example, if you bought an item for $4.80 and sold it for $10.00, your gross profit or margin would be $5.20 and your markup would be 52 percent.

Cost	+	Markup	= Selling price
$4.80	+	$5.20	= $10.00
48%	+	52%	= 100%

The concept of margin is a useful benchmark that will let you compare your business with any other business that uses the retail method. Because margin is expressed as a percentage of selling price, it always means the same thing.

While we are discussing margin, there is another term you should know. In the context of a retail business, *keystone* means that the selling price is exactly double the cost price. You take whatever you pay for an item, double it, and that becomes the selling price. In our sample Monthly Maintained Margin Report, the beginning inventory for this classification would be

SAMPLE 5
MONTHLY MAINTAINED MARGIN REPORT

Line		Cost	Selling
1	Beginning inventory	$25,000	$62,000
2	Receipts (NLC)	12,000	24,000
3	Markups taken		1,000
4	Inventory to be accounted for	$37,000	$87,000

$$5 \quad \text{Markup on inventory} = \frac{\text{selling} - \text{cost}}{\text{selling}} = \frac{\text{profit}}{\text{selling}} = \frac{\$87,000 - \$37,000}{\$87,000} = \frac{\$50,000}{\$87,000} = 57.5\%$$

6 Maintained margin:

		Selling
	Gross sales	$21,000
	Less returns	1,000
	Net sales	$20,000

Inventory reductions for the month:

Line		Selling
	Net sales	$20,000
7	Allowances/Write-offs	500
8	Regular markdowns	2,000
9	Promotional markdowns	1,500
10	Employee discounts	500
11	Shrink reserve (1% of sales is common)	200
12	Total inventory reductions	$24,700

13 Cost of goods sold:

100% − markup on inventory % = cost %   100% − 57.5% = 42.5%

Total inventory reductions × cost % = cost of goods sold $24,700 × 42.5% = $10,497.50

Monthly maintained margin:

Net sales − cost of goods sold = monthly maintained margin $20,000 − $10,497.50 = $9,502.50 = 47.5%

14 Closing inventory:

		Cost	Selling
	Inventory to be accounted for	$37,000.00	$87,000.00
	Cost of goods sold	$10,497.50	
	Inventory reductions at selling		$24,700.00
	Total inventory to be accounted for	$26,502.50	$62,300.00

$$15 \quad \text{Markup on inventory} = \frac{\text{selling} - \text{cost}}{\text{selling}} = \frac{\text{profit}}{\text{selling}} = \frac{\$62,300 - \$26,503}{\$62,300} = \frac{\$35,797}{\$62,300} = 57.5\%$$

$50,000 at selling if we were planning the entire classification on a keystone margin — which we are not.

Line 2 of the monthly maintained margin report accounts for the merchandise received during the month in this classification. The sample shows receipts of $12,000 at cost this month and indicates that these items had been ticketed to sell for $24,000, exactly double the cost price — in this case, a keystone margin.

Line 3 indicates markups. During the month, certain items in the inventory were identified for markup. This means the price could be increased, perhaps because the competition was offering the items at a higher price or because there was no competition for those items.

When you mark up an item in your inventory, you remove the old price ticket and put on a new price ticket that shows a higher selling price. Think about this. You are not changing the cost price of the item — you still paid whatever you paid for it — you are just increasing the selling price.

a word to the wise

The ability to take markups is an important advantage of using the retail method in your accounting instead of a cost method. Although you can take a markdown and reduce the price of an item under either method, you cannot legally take a markup on existing inventory if you use a cost method.

Line 4 shows the result of adding these three figures: a number called *inventory to be accounted for*. In Sample 5, this is $37,000 at cost and $87,000 at selling price. In theory, if you were to add up the price tickets on all of the items in this classification, you would arrive at this number.

As an aside, you should always be thinking in terms of selling price or retail value. Always "buy at retail" — what the customer will pay for the item. It does not matter what you are going to pay for the item initially. It only matters what you can sell it for.

Markup on inventory (Line 5) is a theoretical number that includes the potential profit you would make if you sold all of the items in your inventory at the current selling price. In reality, this will never happen.

The formula for calculating your markup on inventory is selling minus cost (which equals profit), divided by selling. In the sample, this is $87,000 minus $37,000, divided by $87,000, which equals 57.5 percent. This amount is typical for a fashion retailer but extremely high for a hard-goods retailer.

$$\frac{\text{(Selling price} - \text{Cost)}}{\text{Selling price}} = \frac{\text{Profit}}{\text{Selling price}} = \text{Markup on inventory}$$

$$\frac{(\$87{,}000 - \$37{,}000)}{\$87{,}000} = \frac{\$50{,}000}{\$87{,}000} = 57.5\%$$

Line 6 shows the next step: calculating the *maintained margin*. You start by listing your gross sales and subtracting any returns from customers to calculate net sales. In Sample 5, this is $21,000 in gross sales minus $1,000 in returns, leaving $20,000 in net sales. Net sales represent the largest inventory reduction.

Some retailers group the next four items (Lines 7, 8, 9, and 10) into one line, but we recommend that you track them separately. Doing so will let you manage your inventory more effectively and help you make more informed buying decisions.

An allowance (Line 7) sometimes has more descriptive names, including "scratch-and-dent" and "missing button." The idea is this: a customer comes up to your counter and says, "I want to buy this sweater but it has a missing button." To save the sale, you say something like, "Sorry about that. What if I take $5 off the price to compensate you for having to replace the button?"

You need to account for allowances separately so that you can look back in your records and identify problems. For example, you might learn about the quality of a specific item, the packaging used by a certain vendor, or the selling abilities of a particular sales associate.

Good retailers age their inventory. They keep track of how long each item is in their store. We suggest you view inventory that is in your store for three months or less as *current*; between four months and six months as *stale*; and more than six months as *old*.

By striving to have nothing in your store that is more than a year old, you will help protect the net worth of your company. You do this by not having your capital locked into a depreciating asset — your inventory.

a word to the wise

By not buying a particular item in your store, your customers are in essence telling you that your baby is ugly. There is no reason — unless you are selling wine or running an art gallery — to have anything in your inventory that is more than a year old. Among other things, keeping old items in your store is bad customer service, cheating your customers out of being able to buy items that they do want.

You can help encourage the sale of certain items in your store by decreasing their price or by taking a markdown. You should take two kinds of markdowns in your business: *regular* and *promotional*.

Regular markdowns (Line 8) are permanent reductions to the value of your inventory. Promotional markdowns (Line 9) are taken only at the time of sale and available only for a specific length of time. Markdowns are discussed in more detail later in this chapter.

Employee discounts (Line 10) are the price reductions you may offer to people who work in your store. Offering these discounts will let your sales associates try products themselves to gain crucial product knowledge they can then use in their selling.

Both the IRS and Canada Revenue Agency will let you reserve 1 percent of your net sales against *shrinkage* (Line 11). This is the difference between the book value of the inventory that should be in your store and the actual physical inventory. Shrinkage occurs when someone steals an item from your store or you make a paperwork or counting error. You can reserve more than 1 percent for shrinkage if you have historical proof that shrinkage is higher than 1 percent in your store.

On the monthly maintained margin report, the total inventory reductions for the period are calculated at Line 12. This represents the selling price value that left the store. In this sample, the figure was $24,700 for the month.

Next, the calculation of the cost of the merchandise that sold (Line 13) is made. The formula is cost equals selling price minus markup on inventory. In this sample, this is 100 percent minus 57.5 percent, which equals 42.5 percent.

Cost as a percent of selling	=	Selling price	–	Markup on inventory
Cost as a percent of selling	=	100%	–	57.5%
	=	42.5%		

The cost of goods sold is the total inventory reductions for the period multiplied by cost as a percentage. In this sample, cost of goods sold is $24,700 multiplied by 42.5 percent equals $10,497.50.

Cost of goods sold	=	Total inventory reductions	x	Cost as a percentage
Cost of goods sold	=	$24,700.00	x	42.5%
	=	$10,497.50		

To calculate the monthly maintained margin, use the formula net sales minus cost of goods sold equals monthly maintained margin. In this example, it is $20,000.00 minus $10,497.50 to equal $9,502.50.

Monthly maintained margin	=	Net sales	–	Cost of goods sold
Monthly maintained margin	=	$20,000.00	–	$10,497.50
	=	$9,502.50		

To determine the monthly maintained margin as a percentage, divide the monthly maintained margin by net sales. In this example, it is $9,502.50 divided by $20,000.00 to equal 47.5 percent.

$$\text{Monthly maintained margin percent} = \frac{\text{Monthly maintained margin}}{\text{Net sales}}$$

$$\text{Monthly maintained margin percent} = \frac{\$\,9,502.50}{\$20,000.00}$$

$$= 47.5\%$$

In the sample monthly maintained margin report, an initial 57.5 percent markup on inventory eroded into a 47.5 percent maintained margin because of the allowances and discounts given and markdowns taken. If the breakeven point for your business was 35 percent, however, you would be showing a net profit of 12.5 percent and would, consequently, be a very happy retailer. As you will remember from Chapter 1, your breakeven point is the percentage of net sales that it takes to cover all of the expenses of your business except the cost of merchandise. In your first year of operation, you will need to use an estimate. After that, it is a number your accountant can calculate easily.

The final step is to reset the inventory (Line 14). In this example, the $37,000.00 at cost is taken and you then subtract the $10,497.50 cost of goods sold for the period. This gives your total inventory to be accounted for at the end of the period: $26,502.50 at cost.

Total inventory to be accounted for at cost	=	Opening inventory at cost	−	Cost of goods sold for the period at cost
Total inventory to be accounted for at cost	=	$37,000.00	−	$10,497.50
	=	$26,502.50		

You would also take the $87,000 at selling price you started with and subtract the $24,700 cost of goods sold for the period at selling price. This also gives your total inventory to be accounted for at the end of the period — $62,300 at selling price.

Total inventory to be accounted for at selling	=	Opening inventory at selling	−	Cost of goods sold for the period at selling
Total inventory to be accounted for at selling	=	$87,000.00	−	$24,700.00
	=	$62,300.00		

Finally, you again calculate your markup on inventory using the same formula as before (Line 15). You may recall that selling price minus cost equals profit. Profit divided by selling price is your markup. In this example, this would be $62,300 minus $26,503, divided by $62,300, which equals 57.5 percent.

$$\text{Markup on inventory} = \frac{\text{Selling price} - \text{Cost}}{\text{Selling price}} = \frac{\text{Profit}}{\text{Selling price}}$$

$$\text{Markup on inventory} = \frac{\$62,300 - \$26,503}{\$62,300} = \frac{\$35,797}{\$62,300}$$

$$57.5\%$$

Your inventory always resets to the same markup on inventory that you began with. If it does not, you did something wrong. This is because the retail method always accounts for a loss in the month in which it occurs.

On the CD-ROM we have included an Excel spreadsheet that will help you with maintained margin calculations.

The difference between your markup on inventory and your breakeven point tells you how much room you have to keep your inventory current by taking markdowns. If your markup on inventory is 57.5 percent and your breakeven point is 35 percent, you have some room to take markdowns and clear out old inventory. But if your markup on inventory is 57.5 percent and your breakeven point is 55.8 percent, you have very little room. The problem is, if you do not take markdowns and clear out old stock, your inventory will become older and moldier and worth even less.

Controlling Your Business with Four Key Operating Ratios

As you start to bring a level of control to your business (usually in the second year of operation), you will find that an understanding of four key operating ratios is extremely important. These ratios are turnover, stock-to-sales, gross margin return on inventory investment, and sales per square foot.

1. Turnover

Your turnover ratio is something you should review every week. The higher your turnover is, the stronger your retail business will be. With a high turnover, you will have less money invested in your inventory at any given time and a lower risk of carrying items that your customers do not want to buy. You can also get higher sales from the same amount of space, have fresher products in your store, and always be showing something new to tempt your customers.

As you think through plans for your store, you must decide which of the two basic product strategies you will follow:

1. High margin, high price, and low turnover

or

2. Low margin, low price, and high turnover

These strategies are very different. A low turnover item must give you high margin and high price. It has to pay its rent for sitting on your shelf for so long. By contrast, a high turnover item does not need to pay as much rent because another one like it will be along shortly to share the load.

You can mix these two product strategies a little — as long as one is clearly dominant. For example, you might decide to build your business around selling low margin, low price, and high turnover items but choose to stock a few high margin, high price, and low turnover related items as a service to your customers.

If you are running a toy store, this might mean that you decide to build your business around selling popular name-brand dolls and accessories but choose to stock a few dollhouses so your customers can consider a more complete purchase. You would expect to sell mostly dolls and accessories because the dolls are the low margin, low price, and high turnover items that fit with your basic product strategy. The dollhouses are the high margin, high price, and low turnover items that you stock as a service.

The trick is to recognize that you stock the low turnover related items only as a service to your customers, and that you need to get a higher margin and a higher price to cover the cost of providing this service.

The product strategy you choose has a huge impact on the level of customer service in your store. You will soon figure out that you can achieve high turnover simply by being out of stock most of the time. But think this through from your customers' perspective. If they cannot find the items they want in your store, they will probably just shop elsewhere.

The cost of stocking every item in a store 100 percent of the time is more than any retailer can afford. You need to decide how many times you are prepared to tell the customer that you are out of stock but will have new inventory soon. The challenge is to balance your inventory level against your service level.

do the calculation

$$\text{Turnover} = \frac{\text{Net sales}}{\text{Average inventory}}$$

$$\text{Turnover} = \frac{\$\,350,000}{\$\,75,000} = 4.67$$

Performance check:

Good turnover	=	3
Better turnover	=	4
Best turnover	=	6

What will yours be?

$$\text{Turnover} = \frac{\$\,\rule{3cm}{0.4pt}}{\$\,\rule{3cm}{0.4pt}} = \rule{3cm}{0.4pt}$$

2. Stock-to-sales ratio

Your stock-to-sales ratio is somewhat related to merchandise turnover. It is a second measure of how well your inventory level matches your sales. For example, if you wanted to turn your inventory 12 times a year, your stock-to-sales ratio would need to be one to one. Each month you would have in stock just the amount of inventory that you were going to sell that month.

By comparison, if you wanted to turn your inventory three times a year, your stock-to-sales ratio would need to be four to one. Each month you would have in stock four times the amount of inventory that you were going to sell that month. For most owner-operated retailers, a turnover of three times a year is good enough to run a profitable business.

When your store is open and you can start to get a reading on your stock-to-sales ratio, you should worry if the figure is in the six-to-one or eight-to-one range. These would be excessively high, indicating that you are carrying a larger inventory than is warranted by your sales. You will never be able to carry a six- or eight-month supply of merchandise and still show a profit.

Your stock-to-sales ratio will vary a lot during the year, but it should always be at its lowest during your busiest sales month.

$$\text{Stock to sales ratio} = \frac{\text{Beginning of month inventory at selling price}}{\text{Total sales for the month}}$$

$$\text{Stock to sales ratio} = \frac{\$800}{\$200} = \frac{4}{1}$$

do the calculation

Performance check:

Good stock to sales	=	4/1
Better stock to sales	=	3/1
Best stock to sales	=	2/1

What will yours be?

$$\text{Stock to sales ratio} = \frac{\$\rule{2cm}{0.4pt}}{\$\rule{2cm}{0.4pt}} = \rule{2cm}{0.4pt}$$

3. Gross margin return on inventory investment (GMROII)

In addition to being a retailer, you need to think of yourself as an investment broker. You are starting your business with a certain amount of money and investing it in an inventory that you hope to sell at a profit.

Instead of making this investment, you could have chosen to invest in savings bonds, mutual funds, or a money-market account. If you had, you would no doubt be tracking the return you are getting on your investment. Gross margin return on inventory investment, or GMROII, lets you do the same for your retail business. It tells you how much you are getting back for every dollar you have invested in inventory.

GMROII is the only financial ratio that yields a dollar-answer instead of a percentage — it is *never* expressed as a percentage. GMROII answers the question, "What is my return for every dollar that I invest in inventory?"

We believe that if you have a GMROII of anything less than $3, your business is in trouble. Why? If you get only $1 back for every dollar you invest (GMROII = $1), you are achieving exactly nothing. If you get only $2 back (GMROII = $2), you are probably not getting enough to pay your expenses. However, if you get $3 back for every dollar you invest, you will have sufficient return to pay all of your bills and make a good profit.

It makes good business sense to calculate the GMROII of each merchandise classification in your store. By doing so, you will have the information you need to actively build your business around the classification that is giving you the greatest return. For example, you may choose to advertise that classification more or display your products in a different way.

As you gain more experience with retail math, you will become aware of a basic caution that goes hand in hand with GMROII: it does not tell the whole story. This is because the average inventory at cost figure is a calculated number that is based on the physical movement of inventory. When an item arrives at your back door, the clock starts ticking and it keeps running until you sell that item.

But what about the financial movement of inventory? If you sell in 15 days an item that you bought on payment terms of 30, 60, or 90 days, GMROII will not even pick it up. It will calculate the average inventory at cost from your merchandise inventory log and not show that you have no financial investment in that item.

You need to look beyond GMROII and consider the payment terms on which you buy merchandise (discussed in Chapter 3).

$$\text{GMROII} = \frac{\text{Gross margin in dollars}}{\text{Average inventory at cost}}$$

$$\text{GMROII} = \frac{\$\,140,000}{\$\,37,500} = \$3.73$$

**do the
calculation**

Performance check:

Good GMROII	=	$3
Better GMROII	=	$5
Best GMROII	=	$8+

What will yours be?

$$\text{GMROII} = \frac{\$\rule{2cm}{0.4pt}}{\$\rule{2cm}{0.4pt}} = \$\rule{3cm}{0.4pt}$$

4. Sales per square foot

Another of the often-analyzed numbers in retail is sales per square foot. This is an important way to measure your productivity and efficiency as a retailer. This ratio is standard throughout the retail industry, allowing you to compare your store with other stores.

The underlying premise of this ratio is that space costs money, and not just the money you are paying in rent. You need also to account for money spent on heat, electricity, insurance, and cleaning. If you are in a mall, you can add common area charges to the list. With all of these costs, you need to ensure that every square foot of selling space is paying its own way.

Your total selling area in square feet does not include your windows, your stock room, your office, the area behind your cash and wrap, or your dressing rooms — unless these have mirrors, in which case they help sell merchandise and you need to include them. (This detailed definition is necessary to allow retailers to compare themselves to others accurately.)

If your store has annual sales of less than $200 per square foot, either you have far too much space or you are selling far too little from the space you have.

**do the
calculation**

$$\text{Sales per square foot} = \frac{\text{Net annual sales}}{\text{Total selling area in square feet}}$$

$$\text{Sales per square foot} = \frac{\$350,000}{1,000 \text{ square feet}}$$

$$= \$350 \text{ per square foot}$$

Performance check:

Good sales per square foot   = $250

Better sales per square foot   = $400

Best sales per square foot   = $700+

What will yours be?

$$\text{Sales per square foot} = \frac{\$ \underline{\hspace{3cm}}}{\text{square feet}} = \underline{\hspace{3cm}} \text{ per square foot}$$

USING MARKDOWNS EFFECTIVELY

There will always be a certain risk in trying something new in your store, and your buying choices will always carry a certain risk. You are inevitably going to guess wrong and choose a bad color, buy too many units, or set the selling price of an item too high. Having a markdown budget lets you balance this risk.

Markdowns — reductions in the selling price of particular items in your store — are the tuition you pay for an education about your customers. Every retail business should take markdowns, but there *is* an optimum amount. Taking too many markdowns can destroy the profitability of your business. Taking too few can do the same. The most important thing when taking markdowns is that you learn from your mistakes and do not make the same mistakes again. Just as you plan and budget everything else in your business, you need to plan and budget your markdowns. (We will talk more about this when we discuss your six-month merchandise plan in Chapter 3.)

We mentioned earlier that retailers use two kinds of markdowns: regular and promotional.

Regular markdowns are ones you take to reduce permanently the book value of certain items in your inventory. For example, you might reduce a particular line in which you have only broken sizes, colors, or assortments from $49 to $39. You will actually cross off the old price on the price ticket and write the new price using a red pen.

Using promotional markdowns to stimulate your sales

Promotional markdowns are ones you take for a specific event such as a weekend sale. For example, you might plan to sell 50 of a certain item at $19 instead of $24. You should build your plan to include a promotional markdown of $250 (50 units x a $5 price reduction) on this item, but you will record a markdown only for the items you actually sell during the sale. In the case of promotional markdowns, you do not permanently reduce the price of every unit you have in the store. After the sale, the remaining items stay in your inventory at the regular price.

It is vitally important that you record and track every change from the original ticket price of an item. Computer systems can do this automatically if you change the price in the computer at the same time that you change the price of the item. Without a computer inventory system, you would have to manually record each price reduction on a markdown form.

If the price change is only temporary and the price will return to regular after that — as in the case of a promotional markdown for a weekend sale — you will record a markdown only when you sell an item. The promotional markdown list that you keep beside the cash register for those three days might look something like the following chart. You would fill this in for each promotional markdown you take at the cash register. Most stores would fill in the names and stock numbers of the promotional items in the morning and just enter the units sold with hash marks as they go through the day. The following table illustrates a promotional markdown list.

Date of sale: October 3 to 5

Class	Item	Description	Regular price	Sale price	Markdown amount	Quantity sold	Total markdown dollars
3	17395	Women's shoe	$89.95	$79.95	$10.00	|||||		$60.00
8	19990	Women's hose	$5.00	$4.00	$1.00	||||| |||||	$10.00

To record regular markdowns — also called permanent markdowns since the selling price will never go back up — you should use a *laundry list*. You use this list to record a batch of markdowns, completing one line as you change the price of each group of items. The regular markdown laundry list that you use might look like this:

Date: October 1

Class	Item	Description	Regular price	Markdown price	Markdown amount	Units	Total markdown dollars	Reason
3	11122	Tie	$17.00	$8.50	$8.50	10	$85.00	Ugly
2	98773	Shirt	$45.00	$35.00	$10.00	8	$80.00	Too small

that's a good idea

By using both a promotional markdown list and a regular markdown laundry list, you can keep track of every markdown you take. (Blank copies of both these tables are provided on the CD-ROM.) You will constantly be updating your inventory value and tracking your reductions. You can then use this information to identify bad vendors, colors, or sizes so that you do not repeat your buying mistakes.

Using regular markdowns to adjust your inventory to market value

As you build your six-month merchandise plan — discussed in detail in the next chapter — you will need to set aside a certain amount for regular markdowns each month. We recommend that you always use the full amount you have available to reduce the price of the items in your store that need it most.

When you take regular markdowns, you should ignore the cost of the items. Remember that your customers do not care in the least what you paid for an item. They care only about what they must pay. The whole point of taking regular markdowns is to adjust your inventory to market value — the price your customers will pay.

If you always take your regular markdowns on the first day of the month, you will have the maximum number of days in which to record a sale to offset the markdown. Because you record your regular markdowns by month and by classification, it is quite possible to have markdowns that exceed your sales in some classifications in some months. This is not something to fear if you clean up a problem and learn from the experience.

An old cliché in retail is: Your first markdown is the cheapest. This suggests that when you recognize you have made a buying mistake, you should deal with it. Try to eliminate the problem with the first markdown instead of reducing the item's price a little at a time, thus keeping your mistake front and center for the next six months.

There are a number of formulas that supposedly tell you how much to take as a first markdown, but we do not really trust any of them. Instead, we suggest that you determine the appropriate price reduction by looking at your original quantity, your rate of sale, and your turnover goals for the classification. The idea is to calculate how long this particular item would likely be in your store if you did not take the markdown.

For example, if you originally bought 25 of an item and still have 17 of them left after eight weeks, the rate of sale is one per week. This means that you have a 17-week supply if you do not take the markdown and if size, color, and assortment factors do not slow the rate of sale even more. When you sell the last piece, that item will have been in your store for almost the entire 26-week season.

If you have a turnover goal in that classification of more than two turns per year — and it should be at least three turns or higher — you should bite the bullet and cut the price. Because you paid for the item after 30, 60, or 90 days, you are really looking at your own money, including all of your potential profit, when you look at those 17 pieces.

If you choose the right markdown price and sell the 17 pieces in a week or two, do not second-guess yourself. Understand that you took the right action and chose the right price. Just be certain that you learn from the experience and do not buy that item or that color or that quantity or aim for as high a margin the next time.

It is easy to find yourself in a position where you have more items to mark down than you have markdown budget available to do it. This could be the result of many factors, including:

- *Buying based on incomplete records from past seasons.* Without a good road map to guide you, it is easy to end up just about anywhere.

- *Buying based on the availability of co-op advertising or favorable dating.* You should always consider terms when you buy, but they should not be your reason for buying.

- *Overpaying, which, in turn, leads to overpricing.* If customers feel they can get a lower price somewhere else, they will probably shop there.

- *Buying too many.* Most retailers are optimistic by nature, but you should never buy an item solely on the basis of optimism.

- *Buying from too many vendors.* You should not put all of your eggs in one basket, but neither should you spread yourself too thin. You need to have several vendors for whom you are an important account.

- *Bringing in items too early.* If customers see an item before they are ready to buy, it may have become old news by the time they *are* ready.

- *Bringing in items too late.* As tough as it is, you need to enforce delivery dates and cancel late orders. This matters a lot, because you build all of your sales, staffing, and advertising plans around having merchandise at the time you expect it.

- *Having no plan to sell.* You need to plan exactly how you will sell the merchandise you buy. This plan could include advertising, point-of-sale signage, or perhaps special staff training.

- *Repeat orders on fashion merchandise.* You should make it standard practice never to order additional quantities of a fashion item that sells well. By the time you notice the hot seller, place a repeat order, and receive the new shipment, you will probably be well past the peak interest in that item.

- *Broken sizes, colors, or assortments.* When you see any of these, it is probably time for a markdown because you no longer have a good selection for your customers.

- *Competition.* The price is lower down the street and you have to match it.
- *Soil or damage.* Items in your store get shopworn as people look at and examine them. We describe this as getting older and moldier.
- *End of season.* As you get close to the beginning of a new selling season, you should try to sell every piece of nonbasic merchandise from the current season.
- *Poor display or hidden items.* Every item that you buy should have at least one moment in the sun during the prime selling season. Your customers have to see it in order to buy it.
- *Last in, first out on basics.* A fundamental rule of merchandising basic items is that you should place new products on the shelf *behind* any old products you still have.

Increasing Your Credibility by Using Seasonal Markdowns

We believe that most owner-operated retail businesses should follow a seasonal philosophy when it comes to taking markdowns. This philosophy says that you should give seasonal merchandise in your store extended exposure at full price, taking markdowns only at the end of the season. In practice, this usually translates into a commitment to hold your price for at least 16 weeks.

You cannot do many things in the retail business that will frustrate your customers more than reducing the price of the items they bought last week at full price. The down-and-up movement of prices in retail stores through gimmicky sales has left most customers jaded and distrustful. They give price tickets very little regard because they expect that most items will be on sale sooner rather than later.

Following a seasonal markdown philosophy gives your customers time to see your full assortment of merchandise. They can see the ways that items fit together and get used to new ideas. And you can tell them with confidence that it is okay to buy at full price today because everything will not be going on sale tomorrow.

In fact, under a strict application of the seasonal markdown philosophy, all of the merchandise from a season would go on sale at once — in the last six weeks of the season. If you could buy perfectly, this strict application would make sense. However, no one can buy perfectly. That is why we recommend that you take regular markdowns.

When you do take these markdowns, we suggest that you move the items to a special rack or area near the back of the store. You should never contaminate your regular price selection or highlight your buying mistakes by placing them at the front door. Customers interested in discount prices will gladly walk through your regular merchandise to find the bargains.

To help make things clear for your customers, you should always adjust sale items to specific price points instead of to percentage discounts. This will let you create a $10 table, a $20 rack, or whatever. With experience, you will learn the sale prices that work best in your business, and then you can work those into your plan.

a word to the wise

If you want to build any kind of a reputation for quality in the retail business, you must protect your integrity and not play the sale game. Your prices should fluctuate based on a week-by-week plan that you create at the start of the season — although there will always be minor modifications due to competition.

Once you move into the discount arena, you will be competing against the "category killers" and big-box retailers, and you will almost certainly lose. If you need to lower your prices in order to meet your weekly or monthly sales goals, something is drastically wrong and you should seek professional guidance immediately.

**put it
to work**

We suggest that you pause here to look back over the topics we have covered in this chapter on merchandising. While everything is fresh in your mind, you need to decide how well prepared you are for this part of an owner-operated retailer's job.

You then need to decide what three merchandising issues you can work on immediately, what three pieces of additional information you need, and which three people you should telephone or meet with soon.

How well prepared are you for merchandising? (Circle one.)

READINESS		RATING
Need to hire a consultant	✐	1
Need to take some courses	✐	2
Need to read some books	✐	3
Can handle this with effort	✐	4
Can handle this in my sleep	✐	5

What three merchandising issues can you work on immediately, and what can you do about each of them?

1_____

2_____

3_____

What three pieces of additional information do you need to better understand the merchandising part of your job?

1_____

2_____

3_____

Which three people should you telephone or meet with soon about the merchandising part of your job?

1_____

2_____

3_____

Please transfer these answers to the Action Plan in Appendix 1.

3
BUYING

This part of your job includes:

your job description

- Viewing the products you buy through the eyes of your customers

- Building win-win relationships with all of your merchandise suppliers

- Understanding that buying terms are often more important than price

- Following eight proven guidelines whenever and wherever you buy

- Implementing a price-point discipline to offer a clearer presentation

- Establishing a credit history with each of your merchandise suppliers

- Striving to reach "sell and buy" by choosing payment terms carefully

- Calculating an "open to buy" for every classification, every month

- Forecasting and creating six-month merchandise plans by classification

- Buying the right amount of merchandise with a "just in time" philosophy

where you want to go

Seeing Your Products Through Your Customers' Eyes

As the buyer for a retail store, you have a complex and difficult job. One of the most difficult challenges you face is to stop seeing products through your own eyes and start seeing them through the eyes of your customers.

This change of perspective is crucial because when you look at new offerings from your various suppliers, you are really just a proxy for the hundreds of customers who will later stand in your store and look at some of those same items. In this sense, buying is more about fulfilling a responsibility to your customers than it is about the glamor and power that sometimes comes with the position. Accepting your role as a proxy will help you move beyond your personal tastes and let you start to develop a genuine respect for the items that your customers will like and ultimately buy.

Thirty-five years ago, retail buyers had the luxury of believing that their tastes were somehow the same as their customers'. They could afford to make some buying mistakes because times were good and their businesses still made money. A few retailers can still operate this way, but the vast majority cannot. We recommend that you do not waste your time trying to operate in this fashion. When buying for your store, the fact that you may personally like or dislike a particular item is almost irrelevant. The only thing that counts is whether your customers will like it.

Understanding what your customers will like and ultimately buy is going to be a constant challenge as long as you own your retail business. Customers' tastes change over time. You will always need to consider that they may have moved on from an item in your store that they liked just a week or a month ago to an item that you do not carry.

Great retailers are students of their customers — they constantly study their customers and their likes, dislikes, dreams, wishes, and aspirations. We will talk more about your relationships with customers in a later chapter. First, we need to look at your relationships with suppliers, and show that you have more power as an owner-operated retailer than you probably think.

Building Win-Win Relationships with Suppliers

With regard to their suppliers, the challenge that all owner-operated retailers face when they buy is the reality of power: If you think you have power, you do. If you think you don't have power, you don't.

This is an important concept to understand as you buy merchandise for your store. The way that you view yourself and your power will determine who is really in control of your business: you or your suppliers. If you take the attitude that you are just a small owner-operated retailer, a small fish in the ocean who will buy just $15,000 worth of merchandise from a given supplier this year, you will be right. If you think that you have no power and that you are stuck with the payment and other terms the supplier offers, you will be right again.

In other words, if you go into a buying session with a negative mindset, you will come out with a negative result. You will get what you expect to get.

But what if you go in with a different attitude? What if you adopt the attitude that you —

- are a good businessperson and take pride in the way you manage your business;

- represent small business, the engine driving the country's economy;

- are closer to the end-customers than the supplier can ever be, and you have the facts to prove it;

- view your role as being, at least for the moment, to get as much of that supplier's product in front of the customers as is profitably possible for both of you; and

- are the supplier's customer, that you are paying them for a product and have every right to expect to be treated well.

If you go into a buying session with a positive mindset, you will come out with a positive result. You will do even better if you also understand that you are creating a person-to-person relationship with your supplier, and that this can be a win-win relationship. This is a very different kind of partnership than the "us versus them" adversarial relationship that is too common in the industry.

You may be familiar with the scene near the end in *The Wizard of Oz* where Dorothy and her companions finally stand in the presence of Oz. The brilliant lights and thunderous sounds intimidate them — until Toto pulls back the curtain to reveal not a wondrous wizard, but a rather ordinary and pathetic little man. The message here is not that your suppliers are ordinary, pathetic, or little, but that they are human.

Jim recalls his days as a product manager for one of the largest casual-wear suppliers in North America. His customers included some of the biggest retailers in the country plus hundreds of owner-operated retailers from coast to coast.

The large retailers, of course, bought huge quantities of merchandise. The owner-operated retailers bought smaller quantities, some the equivalent of the $15,000 a year mentioned earlier. Month after month, however, Jim made sure that the supplier's distribution facility first filled the orders from a select few of these owner-operated retailers.

How did these small fish get their orders filled first, before the biggest retailers in the country and hundreds of other owner-operated retailers?

It was relatively easy. They established a win-win relationship with the supplier's product manager — a human being who also took pride in his job, recognized the importance of owner-operated retail accounts, needed the end-customer information they could provide, and wanted to sell his products.

They simply picked up the telephone and invited Jim to lunch the next time he was in their city. It was never anything official but, because these few owner-operated retailers were confident and showed some initiative, they got the best allocations and the most complete shipments possible.

Many suppliers welcome owner-operated retailers today. As retail at the highest levels has become more competitive, suppliers have found themselves with fewer but larger accounts. The loss of any one of these accounts could have a serious impact on their bottom line.

This has led them to discover that small is beautiful and that it makes good business sense to have one or two hundred good, healthy owner-operated retailers as customers. These suppliers *want* to develop strategic relationships with owner-operated retailers who will present their products well and provide the end-customer feedback they need.

Despite this change in attitude, you should take advantage of every opportunity to increase your perceived legitimacy in the eyes of your suppliers. Something as simple as the purchase order you use in your initial buying can provide an opportunity to look and be truly professional. As you prepare for your first buying trips, you will need to decide whether to use your supplier's standard purchase order or create one of your own. We believe that if you use the supplier's purchase order, you will give up some of your perceived legitimacy and perhaps some of the power in the relationship.

Instead, we recommend that you print your own purchase order and include *your* terms and conditions — the standard deal that *you* negotiate with suppliers — on the document.

Think about this from the other side of the negotiating table. As a supplier, would you be more impressed by a retailer who comes to the meeting asking to borrow some paper or by one who presents a professional-looking document that spells out his or her standard buying terms in full?

Most office supply stores sell preprinted purchase order forms. Use these as a model for your own personal design.

For reasons we will explain later in this chapter, we believe that you should show standard purchasing terms of net 60 days or even net 90 days, and an order-cancellation date of no more than 30 days after the preferred shipping date. Every order that you write should clearly indicate an in-store cancellation date. If not, you may be legally responsible to accept the merchandise even if it is months late.

Even if you choose to use your supplier's standard purchase order, you may be able to alter the terms printed on that form. As with any contract, either party can change the terms of the purchase if the other party agrees. This means that any changes to the document become binding only when both you and the supplier have initialed those changes.

that's a good idea

Buying Terms Are Often More Important Than Price

One of the key things you need to understand about buying is that the terms you negotiate with a supplier are often more important than the price you actually pay for a product. Terms include things such as who pays for getting the product to your store, the number of days you have to pay the invoice, and various allowances and rebates that relate to the size of your order.

The wide availability of money for co-op advertising is a good illustration of the way that terms can be more important than price. Every year, most manufacturers set aside a certain portion of their budgets for co-op advertising to subsidize retailers' campaigns that include the manufacturers' products, brand names, and logos.

For suppliers, this makes good business sense. They know that placing some of their advertising dollars close to the point of sale will lead to higher sales of their products. For retailers, co-op advertising also makes good business sense because they can save money on advertising campaigns.

Unfortunately, retailers often do not take advantage of this advertising subsidy, leaving much of it sitting unused.

Being creative is the best way to get co-op advertising dollars. Here is a story of one owner-operated retailer — a golf store owner — who did just that and mounted a promotion that he could not have afforded by negotiating price discounts instead.

Rather than approaching just one supplier with a run-of-the-mill proposal for a quarter-page newspaper ad that would include the supplier's logo, this retailer dared to be different. He approached 10 of his suppliers with a creative proposal for a high school golf tournament, one that would benefit his suppliers, his customers, and his store.

His idea was to invite 500 golfers from 17 area schools to the tournament. The golfers would compete over several weeks and, at the end, each participant would receive a gym bag containing golf balls, tees, a glove, and other promotional gifts from the suppliers. Those participants who finished in the top 10 would receive golf clubs, golf shoes, and other large prizes.

The suppliers responded to his proposal by donating a total of $80,000 worth of merchandise to the event. What did they ask in return? They wanted photos to use in their newsletters and a chance to support the tournament with co-op advertising dollars again the following year.

For the suppliers, this tournament was a chance to put their products directly into the hands of 500 young people who could become loyal customers and buy their products for the next 50 years. For the customers, this tournament was a chance to play a game they love and bask in the sunshine of a little VIP treatment. For the store, the tournament was many things, including an advertising and goodwill campaign that would reap benefits for years.

In short, everybody won because the owner-operated retailer understood that terms — co-op advertising in this case — could add more to the profitability of his business than any price breaks he could negotiate with his suppliers.

Suppliers who support co-op advertising will often give you up to 20 percent of the value of your order in co-op advertising dollars. Many will pay 50 percent or more of the cost of an ad that features their products, brand name, and logos. These amounts are usually negotiable.

The following is a partial list of the many terms that you may be able to negotiate with suppliers. No deal will contain all of these, but you may be able to negotiate five or six of them with your best suppliers.

that's a good idea

- FOB terms
- Returns: damaged
- Returns: in-bound freight reimbursed
- Returns: sharing the cost of satisfying the customer
- Returns: collect return transportation
- Markdown money
- Sales representative visits
- Price ticketing done by the manufacturer
- Fixtures
- Packaging
- Selling aids (tags, instruction sheets)
- Promotional material (package stuffers)
- Vendor promotional program
- Rebates (quantity discount, taken quarterly)
- Promotional goods
- Sample items for demonstration purposes
- Advertising mats (glossies)
- In-store demonstrations
- Product knowledge training
- Partial shipments prepaid
- Free mannequins
- Vendor pays for trip to trade show
- Free demonstration merchandise to be returned after use
- On-time delivery or automatic discount
- Vendor pays for Yellow Pages advertisement
- Free electronic data interchange (EDI) software (see Chapter 6 for more on EDI)
- Link on vendor's Web page to your website

Following Eight Proven Buying Guidelines

Here are eight proven buying guidelines to help you buy wisely for your store:

1. Whenever possible, do your buying when you are at your own store. This lets you play the game on your home field in comfortable and familiar surroundings. If you do your buying by telephone, prepare all of the information you will need in advance and place the call at your convenience. The same is true for email negotiations. (Never answer an email without printing it out and thinking about it for at least an hour. Looking at something on a hard copy versus on the screen has a profound impact on how your brain processes the information.)

2. Understand that when you go on an out-of-town buying trip, you are giving up your home-field advantage. The best thing you can do in this situation is to set a modest schedule of appointments that leaves you plenty of time to think, plan, and shop for good ideas at the leading retail stores in the area.

3. Always take your open-to-buy budgets with you on a buying trip. These tell you exactly how much money you have to spend on each merchandise classification and will help you control your inventory and run a profitable business.

4. Never buy an item when you first see it. Instead, take some time to consider the big picture before you place an order. This could mean seeing everything that is available for the coming season before placing any orders if you are a fashion retailer, or reviewing the items you have already bought or could buy if you sell nonfashion items.

5. Invest in a compact digital camera and photograph every item that you buy or are seriously considering buying. These images will help you remember what you have already bought so that you can coordinate colors and avoid buying items that are too similar. Photographs will also be useful in product-knowledge training for your sales associates as the delivery date approaches.

6. Always be honest and ethical with your suppliers so that you can build long-term, win-win relationships with each of them. Your reputation as a business owner and as an individual is something you should always enhance, protect, and defend. Pay your bills on time

and if you are going to be late, let suppliers know how late. Silence is never a good thing when it comes to bills.

7. When you agree on terms with a supplier — but before you sign a purchase order — confirm your understanding of the agreement by restating the deal: You are going to do this, and I am going to do that, right? Then ask any questions you may have: "Can I get additional quantities if I need them?" "Will they be at the same price?"

8. Keep a supplier book and refer to it often. This does not need to be fancy — just a loose-leaf binder in which you can make notes on every contact you have with your ten biggest suppliers. Make this a complete record of your telephone calls, meetings, and any other contacts you may have. You will be surprised at how often you need to refer to this information.

No matter what you are buying, you always have an alternative to buying that item from that supplier, in that place, at that time, in that quantity, and at that price. The alternative may not be as fast or as easy — it may even require you to learn something new — but an alternative does exist somewhere.

If buying the name brand item from the name-brand supplier is the only alternative you can see, you have put yourself in a trap. But if you have five suppliers from whom you can buy a given product, you can no doubt buy more effectively. Perhaps the alternative is to live without the name brand or to develop sales of another brand.

The trick to buying is making sure that you always have an alternative so that you can push away from the negotiating table and say, "I'm sorry, we can't do this deal."

Implementing a Price-Point Discipline

As you think through your store and start to decide on the specific merchandise you will carry, one of the most important things you can do is to implement a price-point discipline. By deciding in advance that you will carry only specific price points within a given merchandise classification, you will be able to offer your customers a clearer in-store presentation and make your buying much easier.

Although many successful stores use just three price points in a classification — good, better, and best — you may elect to use four or even all five of the following in some situations:

(a) Your *opening* price point might be $29. This would be a specific low-end product that you buy to match the low-price leader in your trading area. Depending on the philosophy of your store, you may choose to ignore that competitor instead of battling on price.

(b) Your *good* price point might be $39. This would be an entry-level product offering good features and quality for a good price.

(c) Your *better* price point might be $49. This would be a slightly better product offering somewhat more features and quality for a somewhat higher price.

(d) Your *best* price point might be $59. This would be a noticeably better product offering significantly more features and quality for a significantly higher price.

(e) Your *top-of-the-line* price point might be $79. This would be a specific product that you buy to offer your customers the biggest, the fastest, or the best. You would stock only a few of these very special items.

a word to the wise

In planning your merchandise mix, you need to be careful that your lowest price point in a classification is reasonable in relationship to your highest price point in that classification.

If the spread is too great — for example, if you stock one wristwatch at $29 and another at $299 — a customer who is looking for either one may not enter your store simply because you carry the other price point.

A $299 wristwatch in the window will give a high-price message about your store to a customer who is shopping for a $29 wristwatch. At the same time, a $29 wristwatch in the window will give a low-quality message about your store to a customer who is shopping for a $299 wristwatch.

The only way to avoid this situation is to plan your merchandise mix thoroughly as you initially think through your retail business. You need to decide exactly which customers your business will exist to serve. Attempting to be everything to everyone is a fast route to bankruptcy.

Establishing a Credit History with Each Supplier

As you start to do your buying, you should not expect merchandise suppliers to give you favorable payment terms. This is because your business has not yet established a credit history with those suppliers. Knowing that most new retail businesses fail because of inadequate financing, suppliers will initially be very wary of giving you 30 days or more to pay for the merchandise you order.

This means that for most of your opening orders — indeed, for most of your first year of operation — you should expect to pay the entire cost of each order before delivery. Some suppliers will accept as little as 50 percent of the entire cost in certain situations, but you should not expect it. Do, however, expect a discount when you pay COD (cash/collect on delivery), as there is no risk for the supplier and they get paid right away. You should get at least a 2 percent discount, if not more.

Whether you must pay the entire cost of each order up front or just half of that amount, it is clearly in your best interest to establish a good credit history as quickly as possible. Doing so could take from six months to a year, but you should then be able to negotiate at least 30-day payment terms with most of your suppliers.

This is not as much of a break as it may at first appear. The clock starts ticking on those 30 days as soon as the supplier produces an invoice, which most suppliers do on the same day as they produce the picking tickets that remove the inventory from their warehouse.

If the supplier produces an invoice on Tuesday, the order will probably be picked and packed on Wednesday, and moved to the shipping dock on Thursday. Depending on how far away the supplier is from your store, you may not receive the merchandise until the following Friday. It could then take you several days to open and count the shipment, enter the items into the computer as inventory, add price tickets, and move everything to the sales floor.

In other words, it can easily take half of your 30-day payment terms just to get the merchandise to the sales floor where your customers can see it.

See if you can negotiate the invoice date to be the in-store arrival date and not the invoice creation date. This could buy you up to 15 more days to sell the merchandise, and significantly increase your cash flow.

Checklist 1 is designed to help you evaluate potential suppliers on six important aspects. (A copy is also included in the CD-ROM.)

CHECKLIST 1
SUPPLIER CHECKLIST

List suppliers here >	Supplier 1	Supplier 2	Supplier 3	Supplier 4	Supplier 5	Supplier 6	Supplier 7	Supplier 8	Supplier 9	Supplier 10
PRODUCT										
Demand: A wanted brand name item, line, title										
Recognition: Ease of sell-through										
Packaging: Effective, environmentally friendly										
Quality: High quality, long lasting, no returns										
Units: Singles, six-packs, dozens										
SERVICE IN TERMS OF STOCK										
Delivery: On time										
Bar coded: Carton, package, and product barcodes										
Quantity: As ordered, all at once, no substitutes										
Peak-time support: Will train staff as required										
Returns: Accepted on defective/returned products										
Special orders: Prompt filling										
SERVICE IN TERMS OF SALES										
Sales force: Calls regularly or as requested										
Knowledge: Knows the product and about common problems										
Information: Has industry, sector, and store performance figures										
Review: Conducts quarterly and annual reviews										
PROMOTION										
Advertising: Creates shopping demand for products										
Co-op advertising: Available and flexible										
Promotion: Wide range of promotional items available										
Support: Will help with demonstrations										
FINANCES										
Pricing: Consistent, good value										
Discounts: Offers clearouts to present customers first										
Terms: Will offer net 60 or extend payment										
COMMUNICATION										
Problem solving: Sales representative can do it all										
Executive: Can reach someone in a crisis										

Striving to Reach "Sell and Buy" by Choosing Payment Terms

The most profitable way to run a retail business is to reach *sell and buy*. This is when you sell items to your customers before you have to pay your suppliers for those items. If you could do this with most of your merchandise, you would have a healthy business indeed. You would be making a profit on the individual transactions *and* earning interest on the money which you would be able to invest until it was time to pay your suppliers.

While most owner-operated retailers cannot actually achieve sell and buy because of their size, we believe that you can and should structure your business with that goal in mind. This is where the payment terms that you negotiate with your suppliers become critical.

When buying, you may be able to choose between various payment alternatives. For example, you may be able to choose between paying *2 percent 30* and *net 60*. The first choice means you get a 2 percent discount for paying the invoice in 30 days. The second means that you get no discount, but have 60 days to pay. With sell and buy in mind, we recommend that you choose the net 60 option.

Anyone who understands interest rate math would argue against this advice. He or she would tell you that it just does not make financial sense to pay more than you have to for an item. This is true if you look at the transaction from a short-term perspective.

We still recommend the net 60 option, however, because those terms will help you approach sell and buy. You will pay a little more for the item, but you will stand a much better chance of paying for it with your customers' money. The higher price makes sense if you look at the transaction from a long-term perspective. As a bonus, it will be much easier to return an item to your supplier if you find a hidden defect before you pay the invoice.

When it comes to payment terms, you really need to decide whether you are in the cash-management business or the retail business. If you are in the cash-management business, have significant cash available to you, and can earn more money by taking advantage of quick payment discounts than you can in the stock market, take the 2 percent 30 option.

However, if you are in the retail business, you should focus on turning your inventory quickly and trying to reach sell and buy. The biggest and the best retailers in the world play the game this way and they are hugely successful. We believe you should follow their lead and take the net 60 option.

that's a good idea

When you open your store, you will probably buy products from at least one supplier in a distant city. Most often, you will buy these products free on board, or FOB. This means that you must pay the cost of shipping the products to your store.

In most cases, the supplier will ship by common carrier at the carrier's standard rate. Let's assume that it would cost $75 to get a particular shipment to your store at the standard rate.

Your supplier, however, likely gets a preferred rate because of the huge volume the company ships. Recalling that the terms you negotiate with a supplier are often more important than the price you actually pay for a product, you may want to ask the supplier how much it would cost to ship the products prepaid.

If the answer is that it would cost $50 to ship prepaid, you should immediately offer to pay $50 more on the invoice. It would cost the supplier nothing more, but it would increase by $25 both your gross profit and your net profit.

Calculating an "Open to Buy" for Every Classification, Every Month

Open to buy is the amount of money at retail value that you can spend buying merchandise. Although you will be paying at cost, we believe that you should do your buying based on retail prices. This is a good way of always asking yourself what the items are worth to your customers.

For example, if you know that you have $301 of open to buy in a certain classification, you should go to market with a plan to buy merchandise that you can sell for $301. As you shop, you will need to convert things to cost in order to understand the impact of the purchase on your maintained margin, but this should come *after* you evaluate the items at retail value.

The formula you use to calculate open to buy is this: desired end-of-month inventory plus sales and markdowns minus beginning of month inventory and on-order. See the following illustration using the February figures from a six-month merchandise plan, which is displayed and explained later in this chapter. (Note that everything is at retail.)

Desired end-of-month inventory	$ 920	(Beginning of month for March)
+ Sales	210	(February plan)
+ Markdowns	20	(February plan)
Inventory required	1,150	
– Beginning of month inventory	808	(February plan)
Open to receive	342	
– On-order	0	(February on-order)
Open to buy	$ 342	

To manage your retail business effectively, you will need to calculate an open to buy for every merchandise classification in your store for every month of the season.

Although your open to buy is the amount of money that you can spend buying merchandise, we suggest that you always hold back about 20 percent. This is especially important if you operate in a part of the industry where you get telephone calls from suppliers offering closeouts or clearances for limited periods. By holding back part of your open to buy, you will be in a position to take advantage of these special offers if you wish.

As a hard-and-fast rule, however, you should not buy any merchandise if you do not have sufficient open to buy in that particular merchandise classification. This rule applies even if the deal being offered seems too good to turn down. Special deals seldom provide you with more total sales. Instead, they tend to replace sales of items that you already own.

As an adjunct to this rule, the fact that you may be overbought in one classification does not mean that you should stop your buying in other classifications. For example, if you are in the hardware business, the fact that you are overbought in hammers does not mean that you should stop your buying in nails. The two are not interchangeable in your customers' minds, and depleting your nail selection will do nothing to sell your surplus hammers.

You should never buy more than a three-month supply of any item. Buying a two-month supply would be better and buying a one-month supply would be best. The world changes rapidly in retail and your risk will be significantly lower if you buy closer to your needs.

The further in advance you buy, the more risk you are taking. We believe that you need to offset this risk through a higher margin and more markdown dollars in your budget.

a word to the wise

Forecasting and Creating Six-Month Merchandise Plans

We often joke that forecasting is similar to driving a car blindfolded while someone who is sitting in the back seat and looking out the rear window gives you directions. But we still believe that you *must* make sales forecasts if you want to manage your business effectively.

One of the important ways that you will use these forecasts is to develop six-month merchandise plans that map out the entire product side of your business. To control your inventory properly, you really need to do your six-month merchandise planning at the classification level. If your store has seven departments with ten classifications in each, you simply cannot do this manually. You *must* use a computer spreadsheet to plan at this level. (We have included a spreadsheet for this on the CD-ROM).

The good news is that using a computer spreadsheet not only makes forecasting at the classification level possible, but it often makes it a fascinating experience. You can try out various hypothetical scenarios that will help you understand what impact the decisions you are making will have on your business. For example, what will happen if you buy the factory pack, which contains 12 units, instead of buying only three? How will this affect your GMROII and your turnover?

From this alone, you can see that your six-month merchandise plan is a crucial document. The bad news is that it will take a lot of time to do it well. As just part of the process, you will compute a monthly open-to-buy budget for every classification in your store. This budget will tell you exactly how much to buy, which is much better than not knowing what to do because you have no plan.

**that's a
good idea**

Most retailers plan their buying based on two six-month seasons: February to July (spring) and August to January (fall). Historically, these seasons developed because the clearance markdowns that most retailers take after the busy month of December rightly belong to the fall season — the markdowns are meant to clear that season's merchandise. (The markdowns are applied to the season that caused them.)

As well, every retailer needs to take a physical inventory at some time. This is a complete count by quantity and price of all of the items in the store. For most retailers, the end of January is when they have the least inventory to count and the fewest customers to interrupt the counting.

Sample 6 shows a six-month merchandise plan, which is actually just half of a full-year spreadsheet. To make this discussion easier, we are showing you only the spring season. Fall is off the edge of the page, but don't worry about that now. You only need to plan six months at a time.

If you are not math oriented, you may find this spreadsheet a bit intimidating. Don't worry about that either. Just follow the line-by-line notes, which explain everything. Keep in mind that the six-month merchandise plan is for one classification only and that all of the numbers are at retail value.

If you consider that you need to prepare as many as ten of these classification budgets for each department — and that you will have as many as ten departments in your store — you will quickly see why you need to use a computer to plan at this level of detail.

We start by plugging in our sales history from last year (*Line 1.2*). Some retailers include additional lines showing their sales history from two and even three years ago (*Line 1.1*).

Line 1.3 is the sales forecast or plan. Essentially, we need to guess what our sales will be in this classification for each month of the season. Most retailers make mistakes with their budgeting by being too optimistic in this forecast. It is better to be a bit conservative and not budget for anything more than a 6 percent increase over last year in a given classification. This forces you to be more conservative about your inventory requirements.

SAMPLE 6
SIX-MONTH MERCHANDISE PLAN

Current Year	Category
2007	1

		FEB	MAR	APR	MAY	JUNE	JULY	SEASON
1.0	**MONTH SALES**							
1.1	2005 Actual Net Sales $							
1.2	2006 Actual Net Sales $	200	225	300	350	375	275	1,725
1.3	2007 Planned Net Sales $	210	230	310	350	380	278	1,758
1.4	2007 Plan % Increase = (1.3 – 1.2) / 1.3 x 100	5.0%	2.2%	3.3%	0.0%	1.3%	1.1%	1.9%
1.5	2007 Actual Net Sales $ 0							
1.6	2007 Increase over 2006 = (1.5 – 1.2) / 1.2 x 100							
2.0	**INVENTORY**							JULY EOM
2.1	2006 Actual BOM Retail Inventory $	800	975	1,005	1,200	1,479	1,200	975
2.2	2007 Plan BOM Retail Inventory $ = 1.3 x 3.2	809	920	992	1,155	1,235	1,112	900
2.3	2007 Actual BOM Retail Inventory $							
3.0	**STOCK TO SALES RATIO**							
3.1	2006 Stock to Sales Ratio = 2.1 / 1.2	4.00	4.33	3.35	3.43	3.94	4.36	
3.2	2007 Planned Stock to Sales Ratio (affects Line 2.2)	3.85	4.00	3.20	3.30	3.25	4.00	
3.3	2007 Actual Stock to Sales Ratio = 2.3 / 1.5							
4.0	**MARKDOWNS**							
4.1	2006 Actual Markdown $	20	35	45	80	100	85	365
4.2	2006 Actual Markdown % = 4.1 / 1.2 x 100	10.0%	15.6%	15.0%	22.9%	26.7%	30.9%	21.2%
4.3	2007 Planned Markdown $	20	30	40	75	90	75	330
4.4	2007 Planned Markdown % = 4.3 / 1.3 x 100	9.5%	13.0%	12.9%	21.4%	23.7%	27.0%	18.8%
4.5	2007 Actual Markdown $							
4.6	2007 Actual Markdown % = 4.5 / 1.5 x 100							

		Feb : July	Avg Season
5.0	**INVENTORY TURNOVER**		
5.1	2006 Seasonal Inventory Turn = 2.1 / 5.1.1	1.58	1.58
5.1.1	2006 Avg $ = Feb BOM 2.1 : Jul EOM 2.1 / 7	1,091	1,091
5.2	2007 Plan Seasonal Turn = 2.2 / 5.2.2	1.73	1.73
5.2.2	Plan Avg $ = Feb BOM 2.2 : Jul EOM 2.2 / 7	1,018	1,018
5.3	2007 Actual Seasonal Turn = 2.3 / 5.3.3		
5.3.3	2007 Avg $ = Feb BOM 2.3 + Jul EOM 2.3 / 7		

		FEB	MAR	APR	MAY	JUNE	JULY	SEASON
6.0	**RECEIPT**							
6.1	2006 Opn to Rec $ = (NM 2.1 + TM 1.2 + TM 4.1) – TM 2.1	395	290	540	709	196	135	2,265
6.2	2007 Opn to Rec $ = (NM 2.2 + TM 1.3 + TM 4.3) – IF (TM 2.3 = 0, TM 2.2, TM 2.3)	342	332	513	505	347	141	2,180
6.3	Transfers $							
6.4	On Order $							
6.5	Receipts $							
	(NM = Next Month; TM = This Month)							
7.0	**OPEN TO BUY**							
7.1	2007 OTB $ (6.2 – 6.4 – 6.5 – 6.3)	342	332	513	505	347	141	2,180
8.0	**MARKUP (Gross Margin % on Inventory)**							
8.1	2006 Actual Full Gross Margin Percent	50.0%	50.0%	50.0%	50.0%	50.0%	50.0%	50.0%
8.2	2007 Planned Full Gross Margin Percent	50.0%	50.0%	50.0%	50.0%	50.0%	50.0%	50.0%
8.3	2007 Actual Full Gross Margin Percent							
9.0	**GROSS PROFIT/G–MARGIN %**							
9.1	2006 Act G-Profit $ = 1.2 – (100% – 8.1) x (1.2 + 4.1)	90	95	128	135	138	95	680
9.2	2006 Actual GPM % MO = 9.1 / 1.2 x 100	45.0%	42.2%	42.5%	38.6%	36.7%	34.5%	39.4%
9.3	2007 Plan G-Profit $ = 1.3 + 4.3 x (100% – 8.1) – 1.3	95	100	135	138	145	102	714
9.4	2007 Planned GPM % MO = 9.3 / 1.3 x 100	45.2%	43.5%	43.5%	39.3%	38.2%	36.5%	40.6%
9.5	2007 Act G-Profit $ = 1.5 + 4.5 x (100% – 8.1) – 1.5							
9.6	2007 Actual GPM % = 9.5 / 1.5 x 100							

		Feb : July
10.0	**GMROII**	
10.1	2006 GMROII = Season 9.1 / 6.1.1	1.25
10.2	2007 GMROII Plan = Season 9.3 / 6.2.2	1.40
10.3	2007 GMROII = Season 9.5 / 6.3.3	

Line 1.5 is where we will key in our actual sales for each month of the current year. We want to compare actual sales both to our plan and to last year so that we can make in-season adjustments if necessary.

Line 2.1 is where we then repeat the process for the beginning-of-month (BOM) inventory by plugging in inventory figures from last year. (The $975 figure in this line under the *season* column is both the end-of-July inventory and beginning-of-August inventory.)

Next, we need to average these seven snapshots of BOM inventory by adding them up and dividing by seven. (This is done automatically by the spreadsheet in *Line 5.1.1*.) This indicates that the average stock in this category was $1,091 for the six months of the spring season last year.

Line 2.2, the planned BOM inventory, is automatically calculated by the spreadsheet if you enter a stock-to-sales ratio at or below last year's stock-to-sales ratio. We'll get to this in a minute.

The next thing to consider is turnover. Although turnover normally is expressed in terms of annual results, nothing stops us from looking at it on a seasonal or even a monthly basis. If average stock for this season last year was $1,091 and sales were $1,725, turnover was 1.58 for the period. Your goal should always be to produce a higher turnover for the equivalent season in the current year.

The stock-to-sales ratio is another way to measure this productivity, as shown in Section 3. Again, we start by plugging in our stock-to-sales ratios from last year. In February, for example, the inventory was $800 in this classification and sales were $200, so the stock-to-sales ratio was 4 to 1.

Line 3.2 shows the power of a spreadsheet. We know that we want to increase turnover beyond the 1.58 achieved for the period last year, and we can do this by reducing our stock-to-sales ratio a little bit each month. For the month of February, we decide to budget for a stock-to-sales ratio of 3.85 to 1, and when that was keyed into the sales plan for February, the spreadsheet automatically calculated the BOM inventory we would need to achieve that — $809 (*Line 2.2*).

After doing this for each of the six months, the spreadsheet calculates that the turnover figure would be 1.73 for the season, a good improvement over the 1.58 achieved last year.

Now we move to markdowns. The first step is to plug in numbers from last year (*Line 4.1*). Here we used the total of all inventory reductions — allowances, regular markdowns, promotional markdowns, and employee discounts — from the monthly maintained margin report.

The total markdowns were $365 for the season in this classification last year, which is 21.2 percent of sales (*Line 4.2*). In an effort to become a more productive retailer, we want to reduce this number, too.

In this case, we choose the months in which we think we can improve and plan to take $330 (*Line 4.3*) in markdowns for the season. Given the planned sales increase, this represents 18.8 percent of sales (*Line 4.4*).

Line 8.1 shows the markup on inventory figures for the six-month period last year. Knowing that we will not have any new suppliers and that we cannot make a much higher margin from existing suppliers, we plan to have the same markup on inventory as last year — 50 percent (*Line 8.2*).

Line 9.1 shows gross margin. We could pick up last year's gross margin dollar figures from the monthly maintained margin reports, but the spreadsheet will do it automatically. It will provide these numbers as soon as you assign the sales, markdowns, and stock-to-sales ratios for each month. The spreadsheet can give the planned maintained margin dollars for this year, too (*Line 9.3*).

The spreadsheet also provides projected maintained margin for the season in this classification, which allows us to immediately focus on the big picture. Once we work through a six-month merchandise budget for all of the other classifications in the store, we will have a projected maintained margin for the entire business and we can compare this projection with our breakeven figure — the amount we need to pay the basic bills — and decide if the budgets created will give us what we need.

Lines 10.1 to *10.3* give gross margin return on inventory investment (GMROII), and *Line 7.1* gives open to buy for each month.

A blank Excel spreadsheet that will help you with six-month merchandise plan calculations is included on the CD-ROM. It contains sheets for up to 40 classifications.

As you begin to forecast your second-year sales, we recommend that you start from your actual first-year sales at the classification level. Based on your knowledge of each classification, you should budget for an increase or decrease as appropriate. You should then total the classifications to the department level and the departments to the store level. This is a bottom-up approach to forecasting that begins with the smallest pieces and works up to the whole.

that's a good idea

You could also use a top-down approach in which you start from your actual total store sales, budget for an increase or decrease, and then divide this adjusted figure into departments and classifications.

The top-down approach would probably give you a more realistic total store forecast, but it might be at the expense of a detailed analysis of your business at the classification level. Because you will need to do this analysis if you are to buy more effectively for your second year, we suggest that you work from the bottom up with one eye on the total store figure as you go.

Buying with a "Just in Time" Philosophy

Once you have developed your sales forecast by month, you must decide how much merchandise you will need to support those sales. As you struggle with the question, "How much is enough?" we suggest that you keep two things in mind.

First, inventory is a depreciating asset. From the time you open the cartons, the items in your store are decreasing in value unless they happen to be bottles of fine wine or limited-edition prints. It can be due to normal wear and tear while sitting on your shelf, which dulls their packaging, or due to changing fashion trends. In either case, the items are worth less as time goes by. This point is especially important for an owner-operated retailer who has the entire net worth of his or her company — in some cases his or her entire retirement savings — sitting on a shelf or hanging on a rack as a depreciating asset. A retirement savings plan is supposed to earn you interest, not cost you money.

Second, inventory is a paradox. If you have too little, you are out of business. But if you have too much, the same thing happens.

A retail cliché is: You can't sell goods from an empty wagon. If customers see half-empty shelves when they enter your store, they may assume that you are going out of business, which doesn't inspire confidence. On the other hand, you can't buy everything in sight and end up with merchandise falling off the racks and shelves because there is so much of it.

Somewhere in the middle lies the right amount of inventory. The balance is critical, and one way to find this balance is to do your buying with a philosophy of "just in time" instead of the more common philosophy of "just in case."

You *cannot* be successful as a retailer if you buy merchandise just in case someone might want it in the color blue, just in case you will not be able to get repeats, or just in case it is a hot summer. This philosophy leads retailers to buy too much, incur storage and handling costs, and run the risk of an item becoming shopworn or going out of fashion before it even gets to the selling floor. Merchandise is not cheaper by the dozen if you find yourself facing huge markdowns because you bought the wrong size, color, or style.

However, you *can* be successful if you strive to buy just in time to replace something you sold this morning, keeping your selection complete, or just in time to sell an item before you even have to pay for it. The just in time philosophy always seeks the shortest distance and time from your supplier to your customer. The more efficient you can make this, the more profitable your business will be.

No matter how much you would like it to be, your crystal ball as a buyer will never be perfect. The closer you are to the season, however, the more you will be able to anticipate your customers' needs. The good news is that many of the best suppliers already understand the benefits of just in time inventory management for both retailers and manufacturers. They know that what is right for you is ultimately right for them.

The amount of merchandise you should buy for your store depends entirely on the sales and turnover you want to achieve. For example, if you want to achieve annual sales of $800,000 and turn your inventory four times, you should start with $200,000 worth of merchandise at retail value.

As a rule, your total purchases for a year should not exceed 120 percent of your annual sales. This is somewhat difficult to track, since inventory is always flowing through your business. In addition, you may bring in some spring merchandise during January, which is technically in the previous year in the retail world.

If your goal is to turn your inventory four times a year, you will not go too far wrong if you never buy more of an item than you will sell in the next three months.

Throughout these last two chapters, we have been discussing mostly bean-counter matters. Do not forget to also look at your figures as a merchant.

For example, if, after bean counting, you find out you can only afford to buy 12 of an item, you should put on your merchant's hat to check if that figure makes any sense.

If you recognize as a merchant that you need 24 of the item just to make a decent presentation, put on your bean counter's hat again. Look at your margins and your markdowns and try to find a way that you can make the larger number work. Buy the 24 if you do find a way. Remember that you must be both a bean counter *and* a merchant.

**put it
to work**

We suggest that you pause here to look back over the topics we have covered in this chapter on buying. While everything is fresh in your mind, you need to decide how well prepared you are for this part of an owner-operated retailer's job.

You then need to decide what three buying issues you can work on immediately, what three pieces of additional information you need, and which three people you should telephone or meet with soon.

How well-prepared are you for buying? (Circle one.)

READINESS		RATING
Need to hire a consultant	✏	1
Need to take some courses	✏	2
Need to read some books	✏	3
Can handle this with effort	✏	4
Can handle this in my sleep	✏	5

What three buying issues can you work on immediately, and what can you do about each of them?

1 _____

2 _____

3 _____

What three pieces of additional information do you need to better understand the buying part of your job?

1 _____

2 _____

3 _____

Which three people should you telephone or meet with soon about the buying part of your job?

1 _____

2 _____

3 _____

Please transfer these answers to the Action Plan in Appendix 1.

4

HUMAN RESOURCES

This part of your job includes:

your job description

- Demonstrating through actions that people are your most important asset

- Developing a written job description for the sales associates in your store

- Listing sales associates' eight most important duties in order of priority

- Identifying characteristics and qualifications needed to be a sales associate

- Setting sales associates' sales-per-hour and average-transaction objectives

- Creating a win-win employment relationship through employee benefits

- Paying sales associates by one of three basic methods or a blend of two

- Following established guidelines to avoid common interviewing mistakes

- Conducting hour-long hiring interviews using a proven five-step method

- Evaluating candidates against your duties, characteristics, and qualifications

Demonstrating That People Are Your Most Important Asset

How many times have you seen or heard a company boast: "Our most important asset is our people"? Probably hundreds of times, because it is a great slogan and few people would disagree openly with the sentiment.

The nice words, however, do not match statistics indicating that one-third of all employed people feel insecure about their jobs. What business owners say and what they put into practice are apparently quite different, given the closures, rightsizing, and outsourcing that have occurred in recent years. This chapter and the following one are intended to help you walk the talk and make the slogan a reality for your business.

We believe that every person you employ should have the job of selling to customers. That is what your store exists to do. This means that you should not employ bookkeepers, window dressers, or technology specialists because these people do not sell to customers.

This is a productivity issue. We will devote most of the next chapter to staff productivity and the ways that you can make your investment in wages and benefits pay dividends in terms of sales. Because the productivity of nonselling staff is always zero in terms of sales, we believe you should use outside professionals — people who work for you on a contract basis only — for the functions that are strictly an expense.

The job of selling to customers has many titles in the retail industry, but we feel most comfortable with *sales associate*. The word *sales* tells the employee exactly what his or her role is in the business: to sell. The word *associate* tells the employee exactly how he or she should do that: as part of a team.

A lot of owner-operated retailers would prefer to use a softer term like *service specialist*, but that would put the focus on what employees *are*, instead of what employees *do* and how they do it. The difference is subtle yet significant.

As you get ready to start hiring sales associates, you will need to understand that not everyone can work in the retail business. There are some square pegs out there that simply will not fit into the round holes your business offers. You cannot take just anyone and mold that person into a good employee.

We cannot emphasize too strongly that your choice of sales associates will be absolutely critical to the success of your business. These are the people who will be standing face to face with your customers and bringing — or failing to bring — money into your business. If you make a mistake and hire the wrong person, it could be a deadly mistake.

This is fundamentally different from making a mistake with your buying. When you make a buying mistake, you just take out your red pen, record a markdown, and learn from the experience. You cannot do the same with your staffing mistakes; labor laws see to that. Termination is an area fraught with legal land mines and, in any case, most business owners hate firing an employee. It is much better for all concerned if you simply avoid the whole situation by hiring properly in the first place.

If you do make a mistake and hire the wrong person, you will definitely lose customers. A poor sales associate may not be inclined to greet customers the way you want them to, preferring instead to slurp a soft drink at the cash register or gossip on the telephone with friends. This behavior alone could end your relationship with a customer who might have had a lifetime value of $50,000 to your business.

A weak employee can also destroy the team spirit of all of your good employees who *are* doing a good job for you. They will quickly recognize that the poor sales associate does not carry a fair share of the load when it comes to getting to work on time, serving customers, helping the other sales associates, and keeping the store clean and tidy. Now this person is aggravating both your customers *and* your staff.

The cost of hiring a poor sales associate is still higher than this, since the whole experience wastes both time and money. You will have invested significant time in training the person and will have paid wages to someone who is nonproductive. You will then throw all of this away as you start over with someone new. Naturally, it would have been much better to hire a good employee in the first place.

Although many owner-operated retailers employ family members and friends, we do not believe that this is a good idea — unless one particular person offers the exact set of skills and experience that you find yourself lacking when you complete the Put It to Work exercises at the end of each chapter. The problems that can stem from having family members and friends in your business are huge compared to the potential benefits. For example:

- How can you deal with people on a business-only basis if they are close to you?

- What will you do if their productivity is not high enough to meet your standards?

- How will they react to the ongoing guidance and additional training you must provide?

- Will they second-guess your decisions because they do not respect your authority?

- How will the other sales associates react to having your family members or friends in the store?

If you find yourself having to turn to family members and friends to make your business plan work, you should probably revisit that plan to deal with the big red flag that is waving over it. If you are not able to pay for professional sales associates on paper, you will never be able to pay for them in real life.

Developing a Written Job Description

The first thing you need to do to start finding good employees for your business is to develop a written job description of a sales associate. The importance of this will be evident if you ask yourself one question: "If I do not know what I am looking for, how will I know when I find it?"

The job description will define the perfect sales associate for your store. It will tell you exactly what you are looking for — sales associates that are as close to perfect as you can get — so that you will recognize them when you find them. It needs to be written down because you need a document that you can refer to, pass around, and measure potential and existing employees against. The job description of a sales associate cannot be a vague idea floating around in your head.

As your business evolves, you will no doubt revise this job description to keep it current. However, you should not use this as an excuse to avoid putting pencil to paper now, even if you just come up with a preliminary sketch.

Sample 7 is a sample job description of a sales associate and outlines the most important elements of the job. You may want to expand on this sample, or you may want to create a job description entirely of your own.

Section 1 of the job description form is the job title. People like having a job title that explains what they do. They find it much easier both in the store and when out with friends if they can tell others that they are a "something." As a job title, "sales associate" has been around for a long time. When it denotes a true professional, as it always should, this title is one that people can be proud to have.

Section 2 provides space for a summary of the sales associate's duties and responsibilities. This will be a thumbnail sketch that you can use when discussing the job with other people, but you will have to work through the next section of the form before you can come back to complete this section.

If you want to avoid needless communication problems, ensure that the people who work for you have a clear understanding of the reporting relationships in your business (Section 3). You must make it clear at the outset that the sales associates report either directly to you or to the store manager if you employ one. In the latter case, the sales associates might report indirectly to you.

Determining duties by priority

The core of the sales associate's job description is a list of the duties in order of priority and the relative importance of each duty to the total job (Section 4). This is the section of the document that you really need to get right, but it is the toughest one to think through.

You should not list a duty that says a sales associate must, for example, be nice to customers. This is not specific enough for everyone to be able to follow. You could waste time in endless debates about exactly what behavior qualifies as nice, and the whole point of having a job description would be lost.

JOB DESCRIPTION OF A SALES ASSOCIATE

1.	**Title:**	Sales associate
2.	**Summary of duties:**	The job of a sales associate is to sell merchandise to customers in a professional and ethical manner, and to function as part of a team whenever necessary. A sales associate has eight specific duties, most of which relate to providing top quality customer service and complete customer satisfaction. To receive a "satisfactory" rating in his or her work, a sales associate must also meet specific sales and average-transaction goals.
3.	**Directly reports to:**	Owner/manager
	Indirectly reports to:	N/A

4. **Duties, in order:**   **% of importance to job**

1. Greet and make customers feel welcome	10%
2. Determine customers' needs	15%
3. Provide knowledgeable presentations	15%
4. Suggest additional items	35%
5. Answer any objections	5%
6. Close sales	10%
7. Send thank-you notes or phone	5%
8. Handle maintenance, housekeeping, other	5%

5. **Necessary characteristics:**
   - Positive attitude
   - Degree of extroversion
   - Healthy ego
   - Empathy
   - Friendliness
   - Goal-oriented
   - Neatness of appearance
   - Willing to learn

6. **Necessary qualifications:** Extensive experience in using store's products
   Life experience appropriate to store's target customers
   Proficiency in math

Objectives to be met in the first three months:

7.	**Sales:**	$91.67 per hour (average for a complete pay cycle)
8.	**Average transaction:**	$55.00 (average for a complete pay cycle)
9.	**Other:**	Complete the store's standard new-employee training program and attain a rating of at least "satisfactory" on each of the eight duties listed above.
10.	**Comments:**	New sales, average transaction, and other objectives will be established at the end of the three-month probationary period and discussed in regular performance-review meetings after that.

Instead, you should list a duty indicating that a sales associate must do something that is observable and measurable in language specific enough for anyone to know what it means. This could be something like:

> Make customers feel welcome in the store by giving them a warm and friendly smile and saying, "Good morning" (or "Good afternoon") within 20 seconds of their arrival in the store.

There could be no confusion about what a sales associate is supposed to do with those words in his or her job description. Just as important, you will be able to tell in a moment if the sales associate is fulfilling this duty, just by watching and listening. This duty is something you can observe and measure.

In our sample job description, we have allotted just eight lines for the sales associate's duties, but as you start to think through this job, you will quickly see that the sales associate will be doing hundreds of things every day. We do not provide hundreds of lines to list these duties because you cannot expect a sales associate to arrive in the morning and start to mentally juggle hundreds of duties.

Instead, a sales associate needs to understand clearly what his or her priorities are and what good performance looks like. Even eight duties may be a lot for a sales associate to juggle, but giving the relative importance of each duty should help to make things clear.

You need to decide what you are trying to achieve in your business before you prioritize the sales associate's duties. If you place great importance on housekeeping, you will have a clean and neat store. If you put great stock in the importance of greeting customers, you will have customers who feel welcome.

We do not doubt that you want to have a clean and neat store. The question is, do you want to have this as much as, more than, or less than you want to have your customers feel welcome? And do you want to have these two things as much as, more than, or less than you want to have customers who buy more than one item because your sales associates routinely suggestion sell? You can see how important it is to decide what you are trying to achieve in your business. You will use up the eight lines allotted for duties very quickly.

Once you have established the duties, you should return to Section 2 of the job description and write your own narrative summary of the sales associate's duties and responsibilities, the thumbnail sketch you will use when discussing the job. A blank job description is provided on the CD-ROM.

that's a good idea

When you define your sales associate's duties, you need to be clear about what you want him or her to achieve. We like the following list of duties in order of priority because it focuses the sales associate's job on selling to customers. The list is based on the steps of the sale presented in Jim's book, *Retail Selling Ain't Brain Surgery, It's Twice As Hard* (Dionco, Inc., 2006).

Duties	% of importance to job
1. Make customers feel welcome in the store by giving them a warm, friendly smile and saying "Good morning" within 20 seconds of their arrival	10%
2. Determine customers' needs by asking a series of good open-ended questions	15%
3. Provide knowledgeable merchandise presentations using benefit statements to explain how the products you are showing meet customers' needs	15%
4. Suggest that customers consider the most logical of all the additional items that could complete their original purchases	35%
5. Answer any objections that customers may have	5%
6. Close sales in a friendly, professional manner	10%
7. Send a thank-you note within ten days to every customer who purchases more than $50 in a single transaction and phone within 10 days every customer who purchases more than $100 in a single transaction	5%
8. Handle maintenance and housekeeping chores in a timely manner plus other duties the store manager will assign from time to time	5%

If you do not know the jargon of retail selling skills programs, the duties in the above list may not mean much to you now. The in-store training that you provide will eventually give your sales associates a common vocabulary that will make these duties both observable and measurable.

Identifying relevant characteristics and qualifications

In Section 5 of the job description, you should list the characteristics that a person must have to do the job. In other words, you will not hire anyone who does not have the characteristics on this list. You need to proceed carefully here because in most jurisdictions you cannot consider age, sex, religion, ethnic background, or sexual orientation when you are hiring. The law recognizes that these do not relate to a person's ability to do the job.

The first of our sample list of characteristics is a positive attitude. It is tough to measure this scientifically, but you will know one when you see it. People with a positive attitude tend to approach things with a "go for it" mentality and usually see life as a glass that is half full instead of half empty. People with a positive attitude make significantly better sales associates than people with a negative attitude.

Next, candidates should have a degree of extroversion — outgoing but not overbearing. Shy people just do not make good sales associates. The job entails meeting new people and building long-term relationships with them. Candidates who have trouble looking someone in the eye will be hopelessly lost when it comes to having the extended conversation that is crucial to understanding a customer's needs.

Third on the list is a healthy ego. The day-to-day life of sales associates involves encountering a certain amount of skepticism and rejection. Customers tend to doubt what they hear, and they often say no. If your sales associates feel okay about who they are and have high levels of self-confidence, they will be able to understand that this rejection is not directed at them personally and they will not get discouraged.

Finally, successful sales associates have empathy — the ability to identify with another person's situation, feelings, and motives. Selling professionally involves asking a series of good open-ended questions, listening to the answers, and responding with an appropriate presentation of merchandise. Empathetic listening helps sales associates choose and present merchandise that meets their customers' needs.

Other necessary characteristics could be qualities such as friendliness, being goal-oriented, neatness in appearance, and willingness to learn. These are not as crucial as a positive attitude, extroversion, a healthy ego, and having empathy, but they are useful characteristics for sales associates.

In Section 6, you need to list the qualifications that a person must have in order to do the job. For example, a person cannot be a lifeguard unless he or she has a certain level of training and proficiency that has been tested and certified by the appropriate authority.

Unfortunately, the retail industry does not have an appropriate authority that tests and certifies sales associates. The skills that a person needs to work in your store could be very different from those needed to work in another retail store. This leaves you — and hundreds of thousands of other owner-operated retailers — on your own to set qualifications.

Again, you need to be careful about the legality of those levels of skill or achievement that you define as necessary qualifications. If you operate a store that sells only high-performance racing bikes, it would be considered fair in most jurisdictions to require that your sales associates have a high level of experience with those specialized machines. A weekend athlete would simply not be able to answer the technical and performance questions posed by your knowledgeable customers.

It would also be fair to require that your sales associates have life experience that is appropriate to the store's target customers. For example, a sales associate selling travel accessories would need to have some personal experience with travel in order to understand the difficulties that travelers face.

It would also be considered fair to require proficiency with math, since your sales associates will be dealing with cash, checks, and credit card transactions. Have you ever shopped at a store where the sales associates got confused while recording a multi-item transaction or could not count the correct change even when the cash register indicated what that change should be? Do you really want to put your customers through that kind of frustration?

Legal issues aside, you need to be careful not to set qualifications that screen out potential superstars. Do people really need a college education to work in your store? If so, you can list it as a necessary qualification, but spend a lot of time asking yourself why before you do. Note that you don't have to find someone with every single qualification on your list; you can always provide training.

You should develop a printed job application form so that every candidate who applies for a job will be providing the same information and answering the same questions. If a candidate has a written résumé, he or she can submit it with the application form but should still answer all of your questions.

The best way to develop a job application form is to visit some of the major retailers in your area and get copies of their forms. These stores will undoubtedly have sought expert legal advice when designing their forms, so you should be able to find out what you can and cannot legally ask in your jurisdiction based on a close examination of what others are doing.

Even after you have done this, we recommend that you ask your lawyer to review your wording.

Sales-per-hour and average transaction objectives

When you commit the objectives for your sales associates to paper (Sections 7 to 9), you lay the foundation for much of the coaching work you will do during the first three months of their employment. (See Chapter 5 for more information on coaching.)

The objectives that you list in this section will be the yardsticks by which you ultimately measure your new sales associates' success or failure. You should clearly spell out objectives for the first three months because that is the standard probationary period — in most jurisdictions, this is the period when employers can dismiss new employees without legal notice, just cause, or severance pay.

This probationary period exists because people make mistakes. No matter how careful employers are in their hiring and employees are in their job searches, things sometimes just do not work out. The probationary period lets either side walk away without penalty. Once the probationary period is over, different rules govern the employment relationship.

As the owner of a business, you must read and understand all of the employment law that applies in your jurisdiction. If the law allows for a probationary period, we recommend strongly that you use it.

Each sales associate's primary objective should be his or her sales (Section 7). You are hiring a person who has the job of selling to customers. While you may want to allow for some kind of a learning curve, a new sales associate must get up to speed quickly to become a productive member of the team.

You should express an employee's sales objective in dollars per hour, since you cannot know for certain how many hours per week he or she will be working three months after starting.

Your sales associate's other key objective is his or her average transaction (Section 8). This is the amount, on average, that the sales associate sells to each customer. Thirty-five percent of your sales associate's job should be suggesting that customers consider the most logical additional items that could complete their original purchases. A sales associate's average transaction is the best indication of his or her selling ability — and this ability might not be accurately reflected in his or her sales per hour.

For example, you may have sales associates who are performing at or above standard in terms of average transaction after three months, but below standard in terms of sales per hour. While the sales associates can improve their average transactions through their own efforts, they do not have total control over their sales per hour. It would be unfair to fire people based on their below-standard sales per hour if *your* buying, merchandising, or lack of advertising held them back.

Other objectives to be met in the first three months (Section 9) could be completing the store's standard new-employee training program, learning how to create an in-store display, and learning how to shut down the point-of-sale (POS) system at night. These are not as crucial as sales per hour and average transaction, but they are worth including.

that's a good idea

You may have noticed that we are not making any distinction between full-time employees and part-time employees in our job description. This is because your customers do not care whether sales associates work full time or part time; they care only about receiving professional service.

This means that all of your sales associates should have the same title, duties, characteristics, qualifications, and objectives. The number of hours they work should not enter the picture.

Getting to this point may take a bit of time, however. If some of your sales associates lack any of your necessary qualifications when they first join the business, you will have to make up the deficit through training, and so it may take some time to get all of your employees at the same level. Once you have done this, you can measure all of your sales associates by the same high standards — and so can your customers.

Creating Win-Win Employment Relationships Through Employee Benefits

We believe that an employment relationship will last only when it is a true win-win situation between the employer and the employee. And the truth of today's labor market is that while almost everybody needs a job, nobody needs a job in your store. You need to sell the benefits of working in your store to prospective employees every bit as much as prospective employees need to sell themselves to you.

The competition for good sales associates is fierce. It always has been and it always will be. You will always be able to find average and below-average sales associates, but you will have to work hard if you want to get and keep the good ones.

In the same way, you will always be able to find sales associates whose life experience is inappropriate for the store's target customers, but you will have to work hard if you want to get and keep the ones whose life experience is a perfect match.

Long before you start interviewing, you will need to think through the list of benefits that you can offer prospective employees. Viewed as a whole, this list must be strong enough to get good sales associates excited about the possibility of working for you. We will start with the "hard" benefits — the ones in your employee benefits package — and then discuss some of the "soft" benefits that can often tip a candidate's decision your way.

Although money may or may not be the most important item in your employee benefits package for any particular sales associate, it certainly is the most visible. You need to pay a competitive wage. You cannot expect to pay 10 percent less than the store down the street and keep good sales associates.

We believe that you should pay an hourly wage that is more than competitive with the wages paid for equivalent jobs — inside or outside of retail — in your area. When it comes to employees, you will get what you pay for. This puts a real onus on you to hire properly because you will only be hurting your business if you pay above-average wages to average or below-average sales associates.

The medical, dental, and insurance coverage you offer could well be the deciding factor in winning or losing the battle for good sales associates. Providing medical, dental, and insurance coverage is not cheap — in fact, it costs a lot of money — but this can be an important way that you identify yourself as a "real employer."

People who work in other industries have medical, dental, and insurance coverage, and we believe that people who work in the retail industry should too. If you do not provide such coverage, it is only fair that the "real employees" move somewhere else to get the protection they need.

You have many other benefits to offer prospective employees. The following list includes some of the things you may want to present as the soft benefits of working for you:

- *Employee discounts*: First-hand product knowledge will really help your sales associates sell. You should encourage your sales associates to use the products they sell by giving them those products at cost up to a certain limit each month and only for their personal use. You should offer a lesser discount for items that they want to give as gifts.

- *A chance to learn*: As an owner-operated retailer, you can offer prospective employees a unique opportunity to learn about the retail business in general and the products you carry in particular. Someone working as a sales associate today may very well want to be a chain-store buyer or even an owner-operated retailer in the future.

- *Fun*: Working in retail can be demanding, so your employees had better be having some fun along the way. We are not talking about late-night parties here; we are talking about team contests, achieving goals, and a few opportunities each season to socialize as a group.

- *Status*: For many employees, status comes from having a job title and business card. This alone is a valid reason for giving all of your employees the title of sales associate and for having properly printed business cards waiting when they arrive for their first day on the job.

- *Flexible hours*: While the extended hours of the retail business were once a liability, today these same hours are just right for many people. If you need a sales associate who will start at 10:30 a.m. or work just Mondays, there are probably several good people nearby who want to do exactly that.

- *Opportunity for advancement*: If there is an opportunity for advancement beyond the position of sales associate in your business, you should explain this clearly. If there is no or little opportunity for advancement, you should understand that not everyone wants to move up in the world and that this has nothing to do with them being good employees.

- *Ethics and quality of life*: As we move through an era when terrorism, war, natural disasters, and corporate fraud dominate the news headlines, many people have reacted by reconsidering their fundamental values. In a survey that asked why people enjoy working for their current employers, the majority of people mentioned things like working in a business where ethics are the number one priority, and where the people have enthusiasm for what they do.

that's a good idea

One of the realities of retail is that you will probably hire at least some students who do not intend to make your business their career. Although these young people may be working primarily to earn tuition money or to buy their first car, you have a lot to offer them besides money.

A job in a well-run retail store also provides opportunities to take responsibility and demonstrate self-discipline. An understanding of customer service and the selling skills first learned in the retail business will be surprisingly useful in every job these people ever hold.

Paying Your Sales Associates

You cannot get good people until you pay good wages, but you cannot pay good wages until you get good people. Staffing your business will be a classic chicken-and-egg situation. We believe that if you want to run a profitable retail business, you must break this cycle and take a stand.

By yourself, you could at best be one-half of a mom-and-pop business, the smallest form of retail that can survive. In that case, you would need to be in the store every hour that it is open and then deal with all of the business-related matters and try to have some sort of a personal life after that.

Even while you are building your business in the early days, we believe you should have the help of at least a few competent and capable sales associates. If you cannot pay them an hourly wage that is at least competitive and still make a profit, you might be better off staying out of the business altogether. The writing is on the wall.

Too often, we see owner-operated retailers who are turning their employees faster than they are turning their inventory. They are caught in a downward spiral of dropping sales and employees quitting because they cannot make a good living, which causes sales to drop even further.

When customers see a familiar sales associate in your store, they feel a certain confidence. They assume that your business must be doing well since that sales associate would not stick around otherwise. If your staff turnover starts to rise, you will need to find out why and work to reverse the trend immediately.

The retail industry uses three basic methods of paying sales associates: a weekly wage or salary; an hourly wage; and a straight percentage of sales, also known as a commission.

A store manager typically earns a weekly wage: you agree to pay so many dollars for so many hours of work. In most cases, the employee's hours of work and earnings do not change from week to week.

A part-time or full-time sales associate typically earns an hourly wage: you agree to pay so many dollars for each hour of work. In many jurisdictions, this would be up to 20 hours per week for a part-time sales associate and up to the maximum number of hours allowed before you are required to pay overtime for a full-time sales associate. The employee's hours of work and earnings may be set or they may change from week to week.

A full-time sales associate in a selling store typically earns a straight percentage of sales. (A "selling store" is one where sales associates engage customers in conversations, determining their needs and suggesting complete merchandise solutions to meet those needs. Anything less than this is some variation of self-serve.) You agree to pay a certain portion of every dollar the employee rings through the cash register. Although minimum-wage laws still apply, and overtime laws limit the employee's hours of work, earnings are open ended and totally dependent on sales. For some people, this can be a strong incentive to sell more effectively.

In an effort to get the best of both worlds, some stores blend these methods and pay a weekly or hourly wage plus a commission. In this case, in addition to a weekly or hourly wage that at least satisfies minimum-wage laws, you also agree to pay a certain portion of every dollar the employee rings through the cash register. Because you are guaranteeing part of the employee's total earnings, the commission rate you pay in this scenario should be lower than the one you pay to straight-commission employees.

Under this "blend" pay system, the employee's hours of work may be set or they may change from week to week, but earnings are always open ended. As with paying wages based strictly on commission, for some people there is strong incentive to sell more effectively.

As long as you stay within the labor laws in your jurisdiction, there is no right or wrong pay system to use in your business. The system that feels comfortable to you and lets you get — and keep — good sales associates is the one that you should use.

One of the advantages of paying straight commission is that you always know what your selling cost will be. For example, if you pay your sales associates 10 percent of their sales, your selling cost will always be 10 percent plus the cost of their benefits.

This can work well for everyone as long as your employees never earn less than the minimum hourly wage for your jurisdiction, usually calculated over a complete pay period.

Working against this is the fact that some good sales associates are truly afraid of working on commission. Although they could probably earn more money on commission, they prefer the stability and predictability of a set wage. There is nothing wrong with this as long as you enjoy a win-win employment relationship.

Following Established Guidelines for Effective Interviewing

After you have thought through your job description for sales associates, developed a printed job application form, built a competitive benefits package, and decided on a pay system for your store, you will be ready to start interviewing prospective sales associates.

Interviewing is not something that comes naturally to most owner-operated retailers. If you have not done it before, you will first need to understand the process and then work hard at improving your skills. The following guidelines will help you avoid the most common mistakes that interviewers make:

(a) *Interview three candidates for each position.* From all of the many job applications you collect for each position in your store, you should select just three candidates that best match the characteristics and qualifications you established in writing the job description. We believe that these three candidates are the only ones you should invest time in meeting.

(b) *Schedule enough time*. The sales associates you are hiring could each bring a million dollars in business to your store over the next five years, so you should be willing to set aside at least an hour to interview each candidate properly.

(c) *Meet in a suitable location*. Given the importance of the decisions you are making, you will need to give each discussion your full, undivided attention. This implies that you will need to meet in a quiet place where there will be no interruptions.

(d) *Put the candidate at ease*. For many people, interviews are a frightening experience. This could be for various reasons. As the person conducting the interview, you will need to help the candidate relax so you can get a balanced picture of his or her potential as a sales associate.

(e) *Ask productive questions*. One-hour interviews go by very quickly, so you should stick to questions that will bring out the information you need to make a good decision. The whole point of holding an interview is to gain employment-related information. If you talk too much about anything else — the weather, for example — you are just wasting time.

(f) *Ask behavioral questions*. These deal with things that the candidates have actually done in real-life situations. All too often, interviewers waste time asking hypothetical questions that deal with imaginary situations — ones where the candidates can easily make up what they think are the right answers. As an example, try answering the following yourself: "How do you think the other sales associates would feel if you were ever late for work?"

(g) *Hide any personal bias*. As an interviewer, it is all too easy to telegraph desirable responses to your questions. For example, if a candidate starts telling you about something that happened in his or her last job and you start to frown, the candidate will know immediately that he or she should switch to a different version of the story.

(h) *Focus on listening*. We know from research that the person who does most of the talking in an interview will view the conversation favorably. In other words, if you do most of the talking, you will think that you had a wonderful interview, but you will know very little about the candidate you were supposedly judging. You should probably talk for no more than 20 percent of the total time.

(i) *Promise an answer in reasonable time*. At the end of each interview, you need to establish what will happen next. Because you are meeting only three candidates for each position, you should promise each of them a telephone call within the next few days. This is both polite and professional.

(j) *Allow time between interviews*. You will need time after each interview to make notes while the discussion is fresh in your mind — and then to let your head clear. When conducting several interviews, it is easy to mix up the candidates in your mind.

The best way to conduct your hiring interviews is to give them structure and always follow a set routine. You should ask the same basic questions of every candidate and hold each discussion under approximately the same circumstances. This will let you be consistent and fair, and help you make meaningful comparisons between the candidates.

that's a good idea

Evaluating candidates against only the necessary characteristics and qualifications on the job description will help you make meaningful comparisons. For example, you shouldn't let superficial first impressions influence your decision too much, and you should listen to all of the candidate's answers before forming an opinion.

You will need to ignore how contrasts can make a reasonable candidate who follows a very good candidate look less attractive. You must also temper your natural inclination to feel comfortable with someone who is similar to you. Each prospective sales associate will offer a unique set of strengths and weaknesses. Your challenge is to have a good understanding of these by the end the interview.

Five-step interviewing

Each hiring interview you conduct should last about an hour. In that time, you should move the conversation through five distinct steps. Because each step serves a different purpose, you should not skip any of them or do things in a different order. The one exception to this rule is if you find yourself meeting with someone who has no real chance of working for you, in which case you should end the interview quickly and politely.

The following are the five steps of a hiring interview:

Step 1: Establish rapport (5 minutes)

Step 2: Make the transition to business issues (5 minutes)

Step 3: Probe the main behavioral dimensions (40 minutes)

Step 4: Provide information (5 minutes)

Step 5: End the interview (5 minutes)

These five steps are explained briefly here — space does not allow a full discussion. You may want to attend a full-day workshop on interviewing or do some further reading before you actually attempt it. Finding good sales associates for your business is well worth the effort.

Step 1: Establish rapport (5 minutes)

a. Greet the candidate. Remember that most candidates are apprehensive before an interview and concerned about making a favorable impression. You should introduce yourself, shake hands, and invite the candidate to sit down.

b. Engage in a small amount of social conversation. Start with something you noticed on the candidate's job application form — perhaps the school he or she attended or a hobby mentioned. The purpose of this is to make some connection, put the candidate at ease, and establish a good climate for conversation.

c. Clarify the objectives of the interview. Outline the basic structure you are following so the candidate understands that he or she will speak first, you will speak second, and there will be plenty of time for questions at the end.

Step 2: Transition to business (5 minutes)

d. Ask an easy first question. The purpose of this is to get down to business, get the candidate talking, and get both of you past the butterflies. Your question might be something like, "What led to your interest in retail?" You should ask the same easy first question of each candidate that you interview.

e. Follow up on one specific point. After you listen to the candidate's answer, you should be able to follow up on one specific point. This is how the interview becomes a two-way conversation. The follow-up might be something like, "You mentioned that you think you would be successful in selling. What experience leads you to this conclusion?"

Step 3: Probe the main behavioral dimensions (40 minutes)

f. Ask about work experience. The most important thing to do during an interview is to focus the discussion on the characteristics and qualifications that you know you are looking for in a sales associate. A good question for someone who has retail experience is, "Tell me about the most difficult customer you faced in a previous retail job and how you handled that situation." For someone who does not have retail experience, you might ask, "Tell me about the worst argument you ever had with your best friend and how you handled that situation." Both questions work because people tend to handle conflict in a set way.

g. Ask about education. You might ask something like, "What subject did you enjoy the most at school? Why do you think you enjoyed that subject?"

h. Ask about personal interests. For example, you might ask, "What special interests do you have? How might these be useful to you in this job?"

Step 4: Provide information (5 minutes)

i. Outline the job using the job description. You should wait until this point in the interview to outline the duties of a sales associate in your store because it is now too late for the candidate to tailor his or her answers to your needs. This is not a trick. You have rightly kept the focus of the interview on the candidate until now.

j. Tell something about your business. Without going into too much detail, provide a thumbnail sketch of the past, present, and future of your business so that the candidate can start to understand what he or she might be getting into.

k. Discuss the opportunity for advancement, if any. We said earlier that an employment relationship only lasts if it is a true win-win between the employer and the employee. You should never promise or imply anything that you know you cannot deliver.

l. Explain what will happen next in the selection process. If you have other people to interview, be truthful and say so. Explain that you will make a decision in a certain number of days and promise to telephone when you do.

Step 5: End the interview (5 minutes)

m. Offer to answer questions. Because you have been speaking for the past six or seven minutes, the candidate may have some questions about what you have said. In fact, a good candidate may have a number of questions about what you have said.

n. Thank the candidate for meeting with you. This is more than just being polite; you want to leave the candidate with a positive impression of your store so that he or she can look back on a pleasant discussion regardless of your decision. You should be careful not to build the candidate's expectations of getting the job.

If things go well, the hour you spend with a candidate will pass all too quickly. This is why it is crucial to spend most of your time on the step that matters the most: probing the main behavioral dimensions. Figure 5 illustrates the breakdown of the interview time.

FIGURE 5
HOW TO STRUCTURE AN INTERVIEW

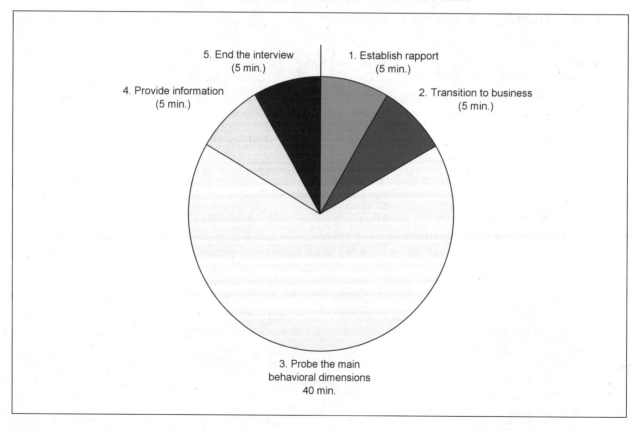

5. End the interview (5 min.)

1. Establish rapport (5 min.)

4. Provide information (5 min.)

2. Transition to business (5 min.)

3. Probe the main behavioral dimensions 40 min.

You should include at least some of the following standard questions in your interviews. As the candidate answers each one, follow up on one specific part of the answer and then return to the next question on your list. Remember to ask everybody the same questions so that you have a good basis for comparing the three candidates you interview.

that's a good idea

- To determine self-motivation and the candidate's capacity for self-supervision, ask: "What individual project have you enjoyed the most in your life and why? What team project?"
- To determine level of aspiration and ability to form goals, ask: "Which interests you more, doing a job well or making lots of money? Why do you say that?"
- To determine self-perception, say: "Tell me three things that would paint a good composite picture of you and help me make my decision."
- To determine appropriateness of choices and values, ask: "Who in your life have you most admired and why?"
- To determine attitudes toward work, ask: "What aspect of this job intrigues you most and why? What do you think you would like the least?"
- To determine whether the person has a good attitude, say: "Tell me about the toughest day you have ever had and what that day was like."

Evaluating the candidates

As soon as a candidate has left the interview, you need to spend some time making notes and thinking through his or her strengths and weaknesses for the position of sales associate. This is the time when the duties, characteristics, and qualifications you spent so much time developing earlier on the job description will make your decision easier. You may find it helpful to use an evaluation checklist like the one shown in Checklist 2. (A blank copy of this form is included on the CD-ROM.)

For each duty, you need to decide if the candidate demonstrated an ability to handle it or not. This may be either yes or no, although you may prefer to use a five-point scale if you are interviewing experienced sales associates.

Next, you should go through your list of necessary characteristics, putting a check mark beside each one that the candidate has demonstrated. You cannot train a person to have these characteristics — the candidate either has them or does not.

CHECKLIST 2
JOB INTERVIEW EVALUATION CHECKLIST

Name: _____

Date of interview: _____

Demonstrated ability for duties:	YES	NO
Greets and makes customers feel welcome	☐	☐
Determines customers' needs	☐	☐
Provides knowledgeable presentations	☐	☐
Suggests additional items	☐	☐
Answers any objections	☐	☐
Closes sales	☐	☐
Sends thank-you notes or makes phone calls	☐	☐
Handles maintenance, housekeeping, other	☐	☐

Characteristics:	YES	NO
Positive attitude	☐	☐
Degree of extroversion	☐	☐
Healthy ego	☐	☐
Empathy	☐	☐
Friendly	☐	☐
Goal-oriented	☐	☐
Neat in appearance	☐	☐
Willing to learn	☐	☐

Qualifications:	YES	WITH TRAINING	NO
Extensive experience in using store's products	☐	☐	☐
Life experience appropriate to store's target customers	☐	☐	☐
Proficiency in math	☐	☐	☐
Other: _____	☐	☐	☐
Other: _____	☐	☐	☐

Notes: _____
_____
_____
_____
_____
_____

Recommendation:

UNACCEPTABLE	FAIR	GOOD	EXCELLENT	OUTSTANDING
1	2	3	4	5

Then you need to work through the necessary qualifications. This will take a little longer because you need to consider each one separately and decide whether the candidate, with some training, could become satisfactory.

Next, you should make some general notes about the candidate that might be worth remembering if you later find yourself with two approximately equal candidates. Quite often, it is the things that you remember at this point — but may not remember later — that will tip the balance in favor of one candidate.

Finally, you should make a recommendation to yourself by deciding where this candidate fits on a five-point scale that ranges from unacceptable to outstanding.

After you have interviewed all three candidates for the job, review your summaries and interview notes from all three meetings, decide on one of the candidates, and then do some reference checks. If everything checks out, you can proceed to offer the job to the most qualified person.

Most jurisdictions will require both you and your new employee to submit various tax forms to the government within a certain number of days of hiring. We recommend that you speak with your accountant to identify and understand these forms, and also that you review the specific employment records that you are required to keep.

a word to the wise

Even with practice, you will not become a perfect interviewer. Eventually, you will probably make a mistake and hire someone who seemed like a nice person but ended up stealing money, merchandise, or both from your business. You cannot eliminate this risk completely, but you can at least reduce the odds of it happening by having a rigorous hiring process and by checking references thoroughly.

Many owner-operated retailers do not check references, but it is not a difficult thing to do. You just pick up the telephone, call the candidate's last two or three employers, explain why you are calling, and ask if they will speak with you.

You certainly want to ask about the characteristics that we have identified as important: attitude, extroversion, ego, and empathy. You may also want to ask about things such as friendliness, orientation to goals, appearance, willingness to learn, punctuality, honesty, and sales ability.

Some employers are reluctant to talk about previous employees for legal reasons. Most, however, will answer one standard question: "Would you rehire this person?" If the answer is yes, you can interpret that as a green light to go ahead and hire.

W e suggest that you pause here to look back over the topics we have covered in this chapter on human resources. While everything is fresh in your mind, you need to decide how well prepared you are for this part of an owner-operated retailer's job.

You then need to decide what three human resources issues you can work on immediately, what three pieces of additional information you need, and which three people you should telephone or meet with soon.

How well prepared are you for human resources? (Circle one.)

READINESS		RATING
Need to hire a consultant	✏	1
Need to take some courses	✏	2
Need to read some books	✏	3
Can handle this with effort	✏	4
Can handle this in my sleep	✏	5

What three human resources issues can you work on immediately, and what can you do about each of them?

1_____

2_____

3_____

What three pieces of additional information do you need to better understand the human resources part of your job?

1_____

2_____

3_____

Which three people should you telephone or meet with soon about the human resources part of your job?

1_____

2_____

3_____

Please transfer these answers to the Action Plan in Appendix 1.

put it to work

5
SALES MANAGEMENT

This part of your job includes:

- Budgeting the wages and benefits you pay as a percentage of your sales

- Bringing productivity to your store through four sales-management ratios

- Using the apprenticeship method of staff training for all new employees

- Providing ongoing guidance and additional training for all sales associates

- Following a sequence of six steps to be an effective coach for your staff

- Reinforcing the bond between a stimulus and the response by praising

- Adjusting training methods to help both personality types cope with change

- Matching goals and incentives to the need levels of your sales associates

your job description

**where you
want to go**

Budgeting Wages and Benefits as a Percentage of Sales

The total amount that you can pay as wages and benefits in your store depends on your total annual net sales. We believe that 14 percent of sales is an appropriate amount to budget for staffing in a typical owner-operated retail business over the course of a year.

You may need to aim for a lower or higher percentage based on the service level you provide. For example, staffing costs should be lower than 14 percent if you operate a self-service store where clerks wait at the cash register, know very little, and simply take money. Staffing costs could be higher than 14 percent if you operate a store offering personal service where sales associates serve customers, provide product knowledge, and truly add value to every transaction. To illustrate:

Self-service	8%
Typical service	14%
Personal service	16%

No matter what kind of retail business you operate, staffing is a productivity issue. You need to get a reasonable return on your staffing investment in the same way you need to get a reasonable return on your inventory and advertising investments. This makes having a good payroll budget every bit as important to the profitability of your business as having good merchandise and advertising plans.

Your payroll budget should include any wages or management fees that you pay to yourself at fair market value. In other words, you need to pay yourself the same wages or management fees that you would pay a professional manager for taking care of your business if you were away for an extended period.

All too often, we have seen owner-operated retailers create payroll budgets that pay everyone else normal wages but leave something like $2 an hour for their own time in an attempt to make their budgets work. This defeats the whole point of doing a budget and wishes away serious sales or staffing problems that the owners should be dealing with.

Given that your annual payroll budget is 14 percent of sales, it would be wise to set each weekly payroll budget as close to 14 percent as possible. By doing this, you will always be matching your staffing costs to your sales. If you get behind on your annual payroll budget during the slow weeks — for example, by paying 20 percent of sales instead of 14 percent — you may find it impossible to catch up during the busier weeks.

To illustrate the budgeting process, look at Sample 8. We will assume that your sales budget is $10,000 for the coming week. Based on your annual payroll budget of 14 percent and a desire to keep each weekly payroll budget as close to this level as possible, you should spend 14 percent of $10,000 or $1,400 for the week. (A blank copy of Sample 8 is included in Excel format on the CD-ROM for your use.)

If the average rate of pay in your store is $14 per hour including both wages and benefits, you could divide the $1,400 by $14 to come up with a budget of 100 staff hours for the week.

Now comes the challenge. In our sample payroll budget, we have taken a first pass at scheduling staff based on the business pattern we expect and the minimum floor coverage we think we need. You can see that we easily used 108 staff hours — and found ourselves wishing we could have more sales associates on the floor at certain times, even though we are eight hours over our ideal.

However, if we followed this first-draft schedule for the week, we would be spending $1,512 or 15.1 percent of our sales budget on staffing. This would be $112 or 1.1 percent of our sales budget above our goal of 14 percent for the week.

One of the biggest mistakes that owner-operated retailers make at this point is to increase their sales budget to bring things into balance on the assumption that a higher level of staffing will somehow result in higher sales. Sometimes it does, but most of the time it does not. This solution *also* defeats the whole point of doing a budget and wishes away serious sales or staffing problems that the owners should be dealing with.

Unfortunately, there is no easy answer here. This is the challenge of staffing an owner-operated retail store. If you reduce your staffing below the minimum floor coverage with which you feel comfortable, you risk serving your customers poorly and incurring losses because of theft. If you do nothing, however, you could be destroying the entire profitability of your business for that week.

SAMPLE 8
WEEKLY PAYROLL BUDGET

Payroll budget for week of: __March 1, 20-- (first draft)__

Sales associate	Sunday		Monday		Tuesday		Wednesday		Thursday		Friday		Saturday		Total hours
	TIME	HOURS	TIME	HOURS	TIME	HOURS	TIME	HOURS	TIME	HOURS	TIME	HOURS	TIME	HOURS	
Pat			10-6	7.0	10-6	7.0			10-6	7.0	10-6	7.0	10-6	7.0	35.0
John	12-5	5.0					10-6	7.0	10-6	7.0	10-6	7.0	10-6	7.0	33.0
Mary	12-5	5.0	1-6	5.0			1-6	5.0	1-6	5.0	1-6	5.0	1-6	5.0	30.0
Jim					1-6	5.0							1-6	5.0	10.0
Total		10.0		12.0		12.0		12.0		19.0		19.0		24.0	108.0

Sales budget __$10,000__   Staff hours budget for week __108.0__

Payroll budget for week __$1,512__   Payroll to sales budget (selling cost %) __15.1%__

Average per hour rate __$14.00__

Note: Hours of work do not include meal and other breaks.

You should do your payroll budgets (and your scheduling) at least two and preferably four weeks in advance so that sales associates can plan their personal lives without conflict or pressure. If you want your staff to be professional in the way they treat your customers, you need to be professional in the way you treat your staff.

that's a good idea

Bringing Productivity to Your Store with Four Key Ratios

As you start to bring a level of productivity to your business in the second year of operation, you will find that an understanding of four key sales-management ratios is extremely important. These are selling cost, conversion rate, average transaction, and items per transaction.

1. Selling cost

Once you establish an annual payroll budget for your store, you will need to look at your sales associates individually to ensure that they are productive in terms of sales. You measure that productivity by calculating their selling cost (wages and benefits as a percentage of sales).

For example, we will assume that you want to achieve a selling cost of 14 percent in your business, which means that you can pay out 14 cents of every sales dollar as wages and benefits. At this level, a full-time employee earning $30,000 a year would need to sell $215,000 a year and a part-time employee earning $12,000 a year would need to sell $85,700 a year to be productive.

A productive full-time employee at 14 percent selling cost:

$$\text{Selling cost} = \frac{\text{Wages and benefits}}{\text{Sales}}$$

$$= \frac{\$\ 30,000}{\$\ 215,000} = 14\%$$

Although the concept is simple, many owner-operated retailers do not explain to their people what being productive means or its critical importance to the survival of the business. Being productive means that everybody pays their own way by generating a certain amount in sales each week, month, or year. There will always be good days and bad days, but, on average, everybody will produce enough in sales over the period to achieve your desired selling cost. If they do not, they are hurting the productivity and the profitability of the entire business.

We believe that you should discuss productivity often with your sales associates and link the wages and benefits you pay directly to it. For example, if a full-time employee wants to earn $33,000 instead of $30,000 a year, that person must *earn* the difference by selling $235,700 instead of $215,000 a year. If a part-time employee wants to earn $14,000 instead of $12,000 a year, that person must *earn* the difference by selling $100,000 instead of $85,700 a year.

No retail business operating today can provide an increase in wages or benefits without a corresponding increase in sales to offset the additional cost. Whether the business is large or small, the profit margin is simply not there to give away.

That said, we recognize that owner-operated retailers in particular need to have happy, satisfied employees who will stay with them for years and help their businesses grow. The only way to achieve this is to pay the sales associates well.

A full-time employee who is selling $235,700 a year is worth $33,000 in wages and benefits to your business. A part-time employee who is selling $100,000 a year is worth $14,000 in wages and benefits to your business. If you pay less than these amounts, your sales associates will eventually move to a store that rewards productivity. If you pay more than these amounts, your business is on the road to disaster.

If you cannot afford to pay people what they are worth, something is wrong somewhere. Perhaps your sales forecast is far out of line, your prices are too low, or you are employing too many people. If this is the case, revisit your sales forecast and your staffing budget. You have to bring these two back into balance.

do the calculation

$$\text{Selling cost} \quad = \quad \frac{\text{Wages and benefits}}{\text{Net Sales}}$$

$$= \quad \frac{\$\ 96,000}{\$\ 800,000} \quad = \quad 12.0\%$$

Performance check:

		Self-service	Typical	Personal service
Good selling cost	=	8%	14%	16%
Better selling cost	=	7%	12%	14%
Best selling cost	=	6%	10%	12%

What will yours be?

$$\text{Selling cost} = \frac{\text{Wages and benefits}}{\text{Net Sales}}$$

$$= \frac{\$\underline{\hspace{2cm}}}{\$\underline{\hspace{2cm}}} = \underline{\hspace{2cm}}\%$$

No matter what pay system you use in your retail business, we believe that you should post everyone's daily sales results in the back room of the store as both recognition and incentive.

that's a good idea

You will not need to add any gold stars, frowning faces, or even make any comments. The sales associates who rank consistently near the top will get their rewards through public recognition.

The sales associates who rank consistently near the bottom will see their positions and start coming to you for guidance and advice. If they do not, you will have learned something important about those people and will need to review their productivity during your next individual coaching sessions.

We believe that far too many retailers regard their people as an expense to control rather than an asset to manage productively. Be careful not to fall into that trap.

2. Conversion rate

Conversion rate is another important measure of your productivity as a retailer. This is the number of transactions you have in a day, week, month, or year divided by the number of customers who enter your store during that same period. It tells you how well you are converting shoppers into buyers and is an important measure of how well you are meeting your customers' expectations and needs.

One of the comments we often hear from owner-operated retailers is: "We don't get enough customer traffic to make a profit in this location." The complaint typically comes from owners who believe they are paying high-traffic rents for less than high-traffic locations.

The problem with this is the implication that the responsibility for generating sales rests outside the four walls of the store — with the property owner. Having high customer traffic is important, but it is probably less important than what you do with whatever traffic you have. In other words, the responsibility for generating sales rests inside the four walls of the store — with you.

To illustrate the point, we note that the conversion rate at a typical 24-hour convenience store approaches 100 percent. Customers go to the store expecting to buy bread and milk and are able to find what they want virtually every time.

However, the conversion rate at a typical specialty store is much lower than that — around 25 percent. Customers go to the store expecting to buy certain items and are able to find what they want only one time in four.

This huge difference between convenience stores and specialty stores suggests that owner-operated retailers can do an incredible number of things to increase sales before they need to worry about customer traffic. Most of these relate to meeting their customers' expectations and needs better, thus improving their conversion rates.

The following table illustrates the importance of conversion rate:

	Store A	Store B
Weekly traffic	600	600
Conversion rate	25% (150 transactions)	28% (168 transactions)
Average sale	$45	$45
Total sales	$6,750	$7,560

With the same weekly traffic of 600 customers and an average sale of $45, simply increasing your conversion rate from 25 percent to 28 percent would lead to a 12 percent increase in your total sales.

Because conversion rate is linked with both the type of store you operate and the location of that store, defining a "good" conversion rate is difficult. If you operate a gift store, your conversion rate will probably be lower than if you operate a fashion store. If your store is located in a mall, your conversion rate will probably be lower than if your store is located on a street. Both of these differences relate to the number of browsers as opposed to shoppers you will have.

Rather than worrying too much about good, better, and best in this case, you should probably just aim to increase your conversion rate steadily from whatever it is now. You can do this by creating a store layout and visual displays that your customers find attractive and by always maintaining a good in-stock position. You can increase your conversion rate even more by having prices that your customers recognize as good value and then adding even *more* value through well-trained sales associates who have incredible product knowledge and know how to sell professionally.

$$\text{Conversion rate} = \frac{\text{Number of transactions}}{\text{Number of customers}}$$

$$= \frac{168}{600} = 28\%$$

do the calculation

Performance check:

		Gift store		Fashion store	
		Mall	Street	Mall	Street
Good conversion rate	=	25%	35%	30%	40%
Better conversion rate	=	30%	40%	35%	45%
Best conversion rate	=	35%	45%	40%	50%

What will yours be?

$$\text{Conversion rate} = \frac{\text{Number of transactions}}{\text{Number of customers}}$$

$$= \underline{\hspace{2cm}} = \underline{\hspace{1.5cm}} \%$$

3. Average transaction

The fastest and most efficient way to get a sales increase in your store is to increase your average transaction. This is the amount, on average, that you sell to each customer. It is a powerful measure of productivity for both individual employees and the store as a whole because it indicates how well you are selling the merchandise you already have to the customers you already have.

We believe that you should explain to your sales associates what average transaction means and then talk about it regularly. (Recall from the previous chapter that we included average transaction in the sample job description.) Many successful stores post this number in the back room so that everyone on staff knows what it is — a goal that staff collectively and individually must meet to be successful. As important, it should be a goal that you will reward staff collectively and individually for meeting.

Focusing your sales associates' attention on average transaction does not mean that they need to become aggressive in their selling. Indeed, they will be much more successful if they simply worry about meeting all of their customers' needs.

In other words, average transaction is about suggestion selling, not push selling. Make sure your sales associates understand that when they look at their average transaction, they are really looking at their own level of selling skills and customer service. And that, by the way, is the biggest difference between a self-service store and a professional-service store.

No matter what your average transaction is in a given week, you should aim to raise it the following week. Whether the number of customers in your store is large or small, the store's average transaction will keep heading in the right direction if you have a concerted selling and service effort by your full team.

The following table illustrates the importance of average transaction:

	Store B	Store C
Weekly traffic	600	600
Conversion rate	28% (168 transactions)	28% (168 transactions)
Average sale	$45	$45 + $10 = $55
Total sales	$7,560	$9,240

With the same weekly traffic of 600 customers and the same conversion rate of 28 percent, the addition of one $10 item to an average sale of $45 results in a 22 percent increase in your total sales.

$$\text{Average transaction} = \frac{\text{Sales for the week}}{\text{Transactions for the week}}$$

$$= \frac{\$\,9,240}{168} = \$55$$

do the calculation

What will yours be?

$$\text{Average transaction} = \frac{\text{Sales for the week}}{\text{Transactions for the week}}$$

$$= \frac{\$\underline{\hspace{2cm}}}{\underline{\hspace{2cm}}} = \$\underline{\hspace{2cm}}$$

that's a good idea

As store manager, you should build rewards and incentives around average transaction. If your store's average transaction was $36 this week, you might offer to pay for breakfast at McDonald's if the team achieves $40 next week.

We suggest McDonald's for a reason — it is probably the best suggestion seller in the country. Try to order just a Big Mac if you do not believe us.

4. Items per transaction

Closely linked with average transaction is the number of items that you sell per transaction. While sales associates can increase their average transaction by selling items that are more expensive, they can increase their items per transaction only through suggestion selling. Because items per transaction measures another aspect of your selling and service, you should track it separately at both the store and individual level.

Some sales associates balk at suggestion selling because they do not want to be pushy. In truth, suggestion selling is really about providing complete customer service — the major competitive advantage that an owner-operated retailer can have in the marketplace.

The concept of suggestion selling is simple. When a customer comes into your store to buy something, that person probably also needs certain additional items that relate to the original purchase. For example, a customer buying a can of paint may also need a paint brush, a roller, a tray, a stir stick, paint thinner, masking tape, a plastic drop sheet, an edger, or brush cleaner.

As a customer service, your sales associate should suggest the most logical of these additional items so that the customer does not get home and suddenly realize he or she does not have something needed to do the job.

As an example, let's assume that the customer also needs a new paint roller and some masking tape. Instead of selling just the can of paint, your sales associate has sold two additional items and brought the number of items per transaction to three. This is a win-win situation. The store sold two additional items and the customer did not have to make a second trip.

Items per transaction is another powerful productivity measure that indicates how well you are selling the merchandise you already have to the customers you already have. Like your average transaction, it should increase steadily, week by week, for as long as you operate your business. If it does not, you are doing something wrong.

**do the
calculation**

$$\text{Items per transaction} = \frac{\text{Items for the week}}{\text{Transactions for the week}}$$

$$= \frac{252}{168} = 1.5$$

What will yours be?

$$\text{Items per transaction} = \frac{\text{Items for the week}}{\text{Transactions for the week}}$$

$$= \underline{\hspace{2cm}} = \underline{\hspace{2cm}}$$

**that's a
good idea**

To avoid any element of push selling in your store, you should encourage your sales associates to suggest first the most logical of all the additional items that could complete the customer's original purchase. If the customer says no, your sales associate should simply stop there. If the customer says yes, your sales associate should suggest the second most logical of all the additional items that could complete the original purchase and keep suggesting items until the customer finally says no.

Suggestion selling is one of the most important parts of providing complete customer service, yet most sales associates feel awkward with it at first. Like any new skill, suggestion selling will take a certain amount of time and practice to master. The rewards, however, will be great — for your sales associates, your customers, and your business.

Using the Apprenticeship Method of Staff Training for All New Employees

Suggestion selling is just one of the many skills you will need to teach your sales associates before they can do their jobs well.

If operating a retail business is your first experience as a teacher, you will find it helpful to know that adults learn new skills most effectively if they first watch and then do. This is why we have included various budgeting exercises throughout the book and the **put it to work** sections at the end of each chapter. After *watching* us paint the picture of where you want to go, you then get to start *doing* — either calculating a budget or building an action plan that will move you closer to your goal.

We are giving you both the knowledge — what you need to know — and some early experience with the skill — what you need to do. The combination of these two will help you start and run a profitable retail business.

If you have ever been to a good skills-training workshop, you will know that this provides the same kind of learning experience. Participants spend a relatively short time watching good examples and then a relatively long time doing role plays and hands-on exercises.

Simply watching the new skill or behavior would not be as effective as watching and then doing — although it would serve a purpose if the participants were watching a good example. It's the role playing and hands-on exercises that really help the participants learn. They need to experience firsthand the new skill or behavior that they are trying to master.

The apprenticeship method of staff training incorporates both the watching and the doing that are so crucial to helping adults learn new skills. This makes it the best method to use in your store. Under this method you view every new employee, or every current employee who is learning a new skill, as an apprentice. His or her job is not to do a complete task initially. Rather, it is to watch and learn from someone who has more experience.

Only after watching and learning for a time will the employee get to try some of the basic components of the complete task. And only after he or she has mastered every one of those basic components will he or she get to try the complete task. At each step of the way, the sales associate will be under the watchful eye of a "master craftsperson" — a person with more experience who can provide guidance and additional training as needed.

If you are a parent, you know how difficult it is to lead by example — to be the master craftsperson from whom an apprentice learns. All too often you find yourself saying, "Do as I say, not as I do."

As the owner of a retail business, however, you will have no choice but to be the master craftsperson. Your sales associates will learn their tasks primarily by watching and listening to you. They will copy and model your behavior at every level. If you greet customers with a friendly "Good morning" as they enter the store, your sales associates will do the same. Much like your children, your sales associates will do as you do, not as you say.

If you have experienced sales associates in your store, you may be able to delegate some staff training to them by implementing a buddy system. Under this system, you pair every new employee or every current employee who is learning a new skill with someone who has more experience in that area. This leaves you free to concentrate on training the trainers.

that's a good idea

If the skill you are teaching is a simple one, some of your sales associates will need just one cycle of watching and then doing to master it. However, you should expect other sales associates to need two or three cycles. Different people learn at different rates. In fact, different people learn different things at different rates.

If the skill you are teaching is a complex one such as suggestion selling, you should expect that all of your sales associates will need many cycles of watching and then doing to master it. Suggestion selling requires an understanding of the way that each item in your store relates to all of the other items in your store. It also requires the ability to ask good, open-ended questions and fully understand each customer's needs.

Suggestion selling, however, is just one of the many skills that your sales associates will need to master before they can do their jobs well. This means that staff training must be an ongoing part of your business — a steady stream of watching and then doing cycles.

Providing Guidance and Additional Training

Under the apprenticeship method of staff training, you will need to provide your sales associates with guidance and additional training in a process known as coaching. This will begin on every new employee's first day on the job and continue for as long as that person works in your business.

Just as you would if you were running a team of professional athletes, you will need to work with the sales associates on your team collectively and individually to get the best possible performance from them.

The guidance and additional training you provide should sound something like: "Good job. I like the way you made that last customer feel welcome in the store by giving such a warm and friendly smile. And if you add the words 'Good morning,' you will find yourself in some great conversations with your customers."

Notice that this coaching contains no negative comments. You need to provide positively phrased comments and then direct your sales associates' behavior in the direction you want it to go.

To be an effective coach, you have to know the game yourself. This includes knowing, understanding, and demonstrating the specific skill or behavior you are trying to teach. You also have to be there to watch and listen as your sales associates first try the basic components of the task and then the complete task. All through the learning curve, your role will be the same: providing guidance and additional training.

When you provide this guidance and additional training in a positive manner, you will be "praising" the right behavior. This is important in the context of staff training and employee motivation because praise is an important reward — and your sales associates will do those things that you reward. We often remind retailers that what gets rewarded gets done.

You will understand this better if you take a moment to recall the many bosses and teachers you have had in your life. We are willing to bet that most of them had an uncanny ability to catch you doing something wrong. No matter how many times you did a task correctly, you always made a mistake right when they walked into the room, and they always pointed it out. We would guess that the guidance and additional training you received from these people left you feeling demoralized, angry, and totally unmotivated to try the task again.

If you have been lucky in life, you may also have had a few bosses or teachers who had an uncanny ability to catch you doing something right. It seemed that no matter how many times you did a task wrong, you always got it right when they walked into the room, and they always pointed it out. We would guess that the guidance and additional training you received from this second group left you feeling positive, happy, and very motivated to try the task again.

All of this leads to an inescapable conclusion: If you hired your sales associates based at least partly on their demonstrating good attitudes to begin with, the responsibility for employee motivation now rests with you. Developing an uncanny ability to catch people doing something right is one of the most important things you can do in your business. If you give guidance and additional training in a positive manner, you will leave your sales associates feeling positive, happy, and *very* motivated to try a task again. Said another way, your attitude and behavior will largely determine whether your store is a positive place to work, with sales associates anticipating each new day, or a negative place to work, with sales associates dreading each new day.

Unfortunately, catching sales associates doing something right is not a behavior that comes naturally to most people. As a business owner, you will need to develop it consciously and practice it constantly. The very success of your business will depend on your ability to become an effective coach and to catch people doing something right instead of doing something wrong.

a word to the wise

In the same way as any coach, you will need to work hard if you want to win. What do we mean by "win" in the context of a retail store? We mean that you will have an incredibly motivated team which consistently delivers results in the form of sales.

As you get better at coaching, you will find that you can bring huge gains in productivity to your business. We have been using the idea of making a customer feel welcome in the store as an example, but this is just one of the hundreds of things you can do to make the shopping experience better for that customer.

You will also find that your sales associates come together as a team under your coaching and that the general level of morale in the store will be higher. As you continue to catch people doing something right, the positive attitude you generate will gain its own momentum, growing stronger and stronger as the months go by.

In this environment, absenteeism will drop. Your sales associates will *want* to show up for work because work is a fun place to be. On those marginal days when they are not totally well, but not totally sick, they may even decide to come in so they do not let their team members down.

Following Six Steps to Become an Effective Coach

We believe that you will need to follow a sequence of six steps in order to be an effective coach for your sales associates.

Step 1: Set goals

You need to set goals for each of your sales associates and these must be measurable, observable, and time specific. For example, you might set a particular sales associate's goal as increasing his or her average transaction from today's level of $36 to $40 in the next week. Once you set the goal, you need to speak with the sales associate often about it so he or she stays focused.

Step 2: Teach the skills

The job of a retail sales associate comprises many separate skills — specific things that the person needs to be able to do. Suggestion selling and the customer greeting we described earlier are both skills. Processing a transaction on the point-of-sale system and sending a thank-you card are skills as well. People do not know how to do these things intuitively. You need to teach them using the apprenticeship method of staff training.

Step 3: Build relationships

We can summarize the third step in three words: trust or bust. Trust is an amazing thing. It takes years to build but only seconds to shatter, and you never really get it back. As a coach, you need to build a professional relationship with each of your sales associates. This is not about being friendly. Rather, it is about being honest and fair with all of your people all of the time in an effort to earn and then keep their trust.

Step 4: Motivate your employees

Giving your sales associates positive reinforcers for appropriate behaviors will create a positive attitude in your business. This is simply a matter of saying something when you see someone doing something right. The closer you can bring the reinforcer to the behavior, the more powerful it will be. Catching a sales associate doing something right immediately is much more powerful than catching him or her doing something right an hour after the fact. We will talk about this more in the next section.

Step 5: Monitor performance

There is not much point to the first four steps if they do not result in better performance. That is why you need to set observable and measurable goals, and then use your own eyes and ears. A few days after setting the average transaction goal in step one, you should be able to look at actual results and see something higher than the $36 starting point. The sales associate does not need to be at the $40 goal yet, just heading there.

Step 6: Provide guidance and additional training

No matter what the sales associate's average transaction is after a few days, you need to catch that person doing something right, provide comments in a positive way, and direct behavior in the direction you want it to go. It is usually best to provide this individual coaching in an informal, one-on-one session. Always be ready to demonstrate the appropriate skill.

that's a good idea

Praise is by far the most powerful motivator you can use, and it costs you absolutely nothing.

Close behind praise is an in-store contest. This can last an hour, a day, a week, or even longer, and the prize can be just about anything. Some sales associates like an hour off with pay so that they can sleep in one morning or take an extended lunch break. We even heard of one owner-operated retailer who was out in the parking lot washing an employee's car, a contest prize that was both inexpensive and fun.

If you want to run a great contest, try passing the buck. You announce this contest at the beginning of the day by holding a quick team meeting just before opening time.

During the meeting, you give one of your sales associates a $20 bill. That sales associate gets to hold the $20 until someone makes the first sale of the day. Because that first sale will be the largest sale of the day, the sales associate that makes it gets to hold the $20. This will go on all day, with the sales associate who makes each subsequent larger sale holding the $20. At closing time, the sales associate holding the $20 is allowed to keep it.

The whole point is to have fun, so don't be afraid to add a little ceremony to the competition. For example, you might add a presentation ceremony and a mineral water "toast" to the victor at closing time!

Using Praise

You may be familiar with a branch of psychology called behaviorism. The basic premise of behaviorism is that for every stimulus, there is a response. Knowing this is useful in the area of staff training because it suggests that we can understand human behavior by looking at the relationship between a stimulus and a response. It also suggests that we can change this relationship by giving reinforcers.

As an illustration, let us consider a customer walking into your store as a stimulus. Your sales associates could give one of several responses. They could —

- avoid eye contact and ignore the customer;

- mumble a halfhearted, "May I help you?"; or

- give a warm, friendly smile and say, "Good morning."

As a coach, you know that you want your sales associates to give the appropriate response: the smile and the greeting. You can encourage this behavior by reinforcing the bond between the stimulus and the appropriate response.

Reinforcers can be either positive or negative. A positive reinforcer would be catching your sales associates doing something right and praising: "Good job. I liked the way you made that last customer feel welcome in the store by giving a warm, friendly smile and saying, 'Good morning.'"

Behaviorism tells us that because humans are pleasure-seeking animals, your sales associates will be more likely to repeat the appropriate response the next time they encounter the stimulus of a customer walking into the store. They will do it to get the positive reinforcer.

If you reinforce the bond between the stimulus and the appropriate response often enough, your sales associates will come to expect a positive reinforcer every time they give the appropriate response. They will have learned that the two always go together.

If you suddenly stop giving positive reinforcers and simply ignore the behavior — that is, you start giving neutral reinforcers — the bond between the stimulus and original response will at first weaken and then eventually die. Your sales associates will learn to expect nothing when they give what used to be the appropriate response.

You can combine these two situations by sometimes giving positive reinforcers and sometimes giving neutral reinforcers in what psychologists call a gambling schedule. The sales associates "win" a few times by giving the appropriate response, then they do not win for a while, and then they win again. Most people will keep trying even when they are not winning because of the chance that they could win again.

You should try to consciously follow a gambling schedule when it comes to giving praise. Your sales associates will then learn that they sometimes get positive reinforcers and sometimes get neutral reinforcers when they give the appropriate response. Most people can live with that.

The important advantage to following a gambling schedule is that you will not need to be present every moment the store is open. Whether you are out on the selling floor or away on a buying trip, your sales associates will be giving the appropriate response whenever they encounter the stimulus of a customer walking into the store.

a word to the wise

Unfortunately, some people will do things to get a negative reinforcer. A negative reinforcer would be catching your sales associates doing something wrong: "I've told you a hundred times not to ignore customers."

This can easily lead to a downward spiral where your sales associates will be more and more likely to repeat the inappropriate response the next time they encounter the stimulus of a customer walking into the store. They will do this to get the negative reinforcer, which is better than getting no reinforcer from you at all.

Adjusting Training Methods

People are homeostatic organisms. This is a fancy way of saying that we live in balance. Most of us do not take a different route to work each day or rearrange our furniture each week. We tend to prefer routine because it is comfortable, and to resist change because it is stressful.

Not everyone deals with stress the same way. People with type A personalities eat stress for breakfast. You will typically find these people moving at a fast pace and exhibiting various degrees of impatience.

In contrast to this, people with type B personalities will *never* eat stress if they can avoid it. You typically find these people moving at a more reasonable pace and exhibiting a composed and relaxed attitude.

The team of sales associates that you build should contain a balance of these two personality types, which means that you need to understand how each is likely to react in a given situation. Note that we are only talking about how people react to stress here. Personality type has nothing to do with intelligence, ability, or motivation.

If you are planning a training session in which you want to teach your sales associates the skill of greeting customers, you need to be aware that this will involve stress. For example, when faced with learning a new skill — which involves changing a behavior — people with a type A personality may find the experience moderately stressful. However, people with a type B personality may find it *very* stressful.

This has some powerful implications. Sales associates with a type B personality may find it very stressful to make the customer feel welcome in the store by giving a warm, friendly smile and saying, "Good morning." They may be able to manage the smile but not the words, or the words but not the smile. You are asking them to do something differently. You are asking them to practice a new behavior, and, until your sales associates have greeted customers in the new manner enough times to feel comfortable with it, the change will cause significant stress.

You may know about this from your own experience. For example, if you have ever taken a tennis lesson, the professional probably taught you to hold the racket with a different grip. You were willing to try until the first time you had to use the new grip in a match. Under pressure, you probably went back to the old and comfortable way.

You did this despite an intuitive understanding that the new grip would have become comfortable if you had just practiced it, and that your game would now be better as a result. You should keep this example in mind when you start asking sales associates to try new skills, and you should work hard at catching them doing something right as they attempt these skills.

Praise acts as a motivator because it helps people keep score. At the end of the day, they can leave with a clear understanding of whether they won, lost, or broke even. For most sales associates, even losing would be better than drifting from day to day without feedback or guidance.

In your role as a coach, you will always need to remember the importance of performance measures to yourself and to others. A retail store can quickly grow stale if working there is not a fresh, fun, and challenging experience for everyone involved. You will need to change things around constantly so that nothing starts to get too predictable.

Matching Goals and Incentives to Your Sales Associates' Needs

Keeping your sales associates motivated may turn out to be one of the most challenging parts of your job as a retailer. We are often asked about employee motivation by owner-operated retailers at our workshops. Perhaps a new sales associate's gung-ho attitude is changing rapidly to a ho-hum attitude, or one of the store's senior people seems restless and discouraged.

The secret to understanding employee motivation lies partly in understanding the work of Abraham Maslow (1908–1970), an American psychologist and one of the founders of humanistic psychology. Maslow developed a triangle-shaped model of human motivation in which a higher need becomes important only after all of the lower needs have been fulfilled.

Basic human needs such as food and water are critical, so these are at the base of the triangle. Safety and security needs are on the second level. The need for belonging and love is on the third level, followed by self-esteem needs on the fourth level. Self-actualization needs are at the top of the triangle.

In the retail business, you will typically be dealing with people who are at either level three or level four of Maslow's triangle. In other words, your sales associates will typically have either belonging and love needs or self-esteem needs. The people in these two groups are very different, so the challenge lies in providing the right kind of motivation for each group.

Affiliation motivation works for people whose needs center on belonging and love. People in this group want most to be part of a team and to be accepted by that team. This is good because it creates synergy through which the team becomes greater than the sum of its parts.

The best way to motivate people who are looking for belonging and love is to provide group contests. You provide just one goal for the entire team. Activities outside the store such as parties or softball games — anything social — will work well with this group. If you employ only people who are interested in belonging and love in your store, you will have a supportive, noncompetitive group.

Achievement motivation works for people whose needs center on self-esteem. People in this group have all of their belonging and love needs fulfilled and now want most to compete and achieve because this will lead to personal growth. This is good because it creates achievement-oriented competition in which people meet their sales targets.

The best way to motivate people interested in self-esteem is to provide individual goals and incentives. You provide individual targets and each person will relish the personal challenge of meeting and beating theirs. If you employ only people interested in competing and achieving in the store, you will have a group of competitive, nonsupportive individuals.

Many of the problems that owner-operated retailers face in the area of motivation originate with goals and incentives that are inappropriate for their sales associates. For example, if you offer individual goals and incentives to people who are at the belonging and love level, they will not connect with the idea at all. If you were to take a belonging and love group and start paying commission in an effort to increase sales, it probably would not work.

However, if you offer group goals and incentives to people who are at the self-esteem level, they will not connect with the idea at all. If you were to take a self-esteem group and offer everyone a night at the movies for meeting a team goal, it probably would not work. When competition is lacking, self-esteem people tend to lose interest very quickly.

The good news is that those sales associates interested in self-esteem will gladly be part of a team if they also get personal recognition. This means that you need to provide both affiliation and achievement motivation in order to cover both groups. Any professional sports team will serve as a good model of how to do this.

Whether the sport is basketball, baseball, or hockey, the individual players win only when their team wins. No matter how dominant the team's superstar may be, that person cannot reach the goal alone. He or she knows that the team must pull together as a unit to be successful. This is affiliation motivation.

At the same time, everyone keeps track of exactly who made the shots and who scored the goals. This is achievement motivation.

The most powerful team you can build in your store is a team of affiliative achievers. These are people at the self-esteem level of Maslow's triangle who understand that the only way they can win is by working together.

that's a good idea

You will probably have some sales associates on your team who are affiliation motivated and do not respond to individual goals at all, and some who are achievement motivated — the superstars trying to emerge. You can motivate this kind of team effectively if you understand that people at the affiliation level cannot participate at the achievement level.

In other words, you need to have both affiliation and achievement rewards in place, but the affiliation reward should be the dominant one. As an example, your rewards might be: "If we make our sales goal this month, everybody will get an extra $50 in their pay. The top two performers in average transaction will get an additional $50 each."

We suggest that you pause here to look back over the topics we have covered in this chapter on sales management. While everything is fresh in your mind, you need to decide how well prepared you are for this part of an owner-operated retailer's job.

You then need to decide what three sales management issues you can work on immediately, what three pieces of additional information you need, and which three people you should telephone or meet with soon.

How well prepared are you for sales management? (Circle one.)

READINESS		RATING
Need to hire a consultant	✐	1
Need to take some courses	✐	2
Need to read some books	✐	3
Can handle this with effort	✐	4
Can handle this in my sleep	✐	5

What three sales management issues can you work on immediately, and what can you do about each of them?

1_____

2_____

3_____

What three pieces of additional information do you need to better understand the sales management part of your job?

1_____

2_____

3_____

Which three people should you telephone or meet with soon about the sales management part of your job?

1_____

2_____

3_____

Please transfer these answers to the Action Plan in Appendix 1.

6
TECHNOLOGY

This part of your job includes:

your job description

- Embracing the relevant trends in retail and Internet technology

- Understanding your technology needs and budgeting for them

- Selecting the right integrated POS/merchandising/CRM package

- Understanding the many things that your integrated package should do

- Using your investment in technology wisely to run a profitable business

- Keeping your inventory, sales, profit, and space in the correct balance

- Making an informed decision about POS software suppliers

- Contacting other retailers to confirm the information you have heard

Embracing the Relevant Trends in Retail and Internet Technology

The rapid evolution of technology has brought dramatic change to the retail industry in recent years. The biggest and the best companies are taking advantage of every step forward to increase their efficiency — which ultimately means that they can offer products to their customers at lower prices, with better in-stock service and increased profitability.

All too often, however, owner-operated retailers choose to fight the inevitable. They avoid new technology and stick with business methods that are at least 35 years out of date. And they are losing the battle for customers because of it.

The advance of technology is like a parade coming down the street. You can either join in or get out of the way and watch it pass you by. In the following sections we will discuss six trends in retail and Internet technology that offer huge opportunities for owner-operated retailers.

Using a computer and retail software as a cash register

Over the years retailers have used various kinds of cash registers to record their sales. These range from what was basically an electric adding machine, which provided only total sales at the end of the day in the 1950s, to an electronic cash register, which provided sales by department in the 1970s. In other words, the "latest technology" did not provide information at a very detailed level.

The personal computer has changed all of this. Once you equip a basic computer with retail software, a bar-code scanner, a cash drawer, a receipt printer, and a credit card reader, it can make the smallest details of your business immediately accessible.

As an owner-operated retailer, the most important of these details will be the ones you get about your customers. By using a personal computer with retail software, you can track their names, addresses, and telephone numbers. You can tie this information to their purchase histories so that you can better understand their purchase frequencies and their needs. Once you have done that, you can communicate with them individually and inexpensively through relationship marketing.

Although you may also find some benefits in the area of inventory reduction and productivity, we believe that the real benefits of using retail software in your business will come through selling more merchandise.

Automatic replenishment

You will make much better use of your time if you let technology look after the simple things in your store — things like writing repeat purchase orders on basic merchandise. Automatic replenishment can do this much faster, more efficiently, and at a much lower cost than any staff person can.

The idea behind automatic replenishment is that once you have established a *model stock* for a given item (i.e., the optimal inventory that balances in-stock position with the cost of carrying it), the computer can do all of the rest. It can constantly monitor the on-hand quantity, the rate of sale, and the expected out-of-stock date for that item. Moreover, it can check this against the model stock and even write a purchase order if necessary.

Although automatic replenishment works best on a basic inventory, many fashion retailers are now experimenting with it. They use a computer program to track the size, color, and price of whatever item a customer purchases, and then have the computer order an equivalent item that is currently available from the same supplier.

This may sound like a small thing, but, as an owner-operated retailer, you will need to find every way possible to maximize your use of time. If you can learn to use technology effectively in an area such as reordering, you will have a lot more time to work on other priorities in your job description.

Multimedia

Given the explosive growth of multimedia in recent years, we believe that every personal computer in your store should have a CD/DVD drive. The cost will be less than $50 per machine, and you will recoup more than that in staff training benefits during the first week alone.

Many suppliers are now providing catalogs and product-knowledge training for retail sales associates on CD/DVDs, and most provide these at no cost. As the cost of creating multimedia drops, more suppliers will no doubt join the trend.

If you have the talent and inclination, you might even want to create your own multimedia store catalog. With the drag and drop simplicity now common to most computer programs, you can take the images and sounds from your suppliers' presentations and integrate them into one of your own. Instead of fumbling through a drawer to find your suppliers' printed catalogs, you can use a touch-screen display to show your customers all the items they can special order through your store.

Multimedia is a whole new way for retailers to communicate with customers — one that no doubt will grow exponentially because it pays big dividends.

Executive information systems

As you may know, corporate presidents often will not take the time to learn complicated computer programs. This is why the software companies that sell executive information systems make them easy to use — and therefore perfect for owner-operated retailers who do not *have* the time to learn. With just a few clicks of the mouse, you can begin learning all sorts of amazing things about your business.

For example, you can see your sales curve for the past six weeks and then overlay your payroll expense or your inventory level for the same weeks. This is easy to do with an executive information system, and the results are presented visually. Because the presentation is so clear, the trends tend to jump off the screen and hit you in the face.

This is a huge step forward from the days when retailers had to create complex database queries and design report templates before they could learn anything about their businesses. That process took hours, and the results did not yield nearly as much information as you can now have in just minutes. If your payroll expense does not match your sales curve — an important issue if you intend to be a successful retailer — you can immediately start to look for the reason and plan corrective action.

Most modern integrated POS/Merchandising/CRM software packages have these report systems built right in. The more advanced systems are adding *dashboards*, which just like your car dashboard, tell you everything that you need to know about what is happening in your business right now. This real-time reporting of data is becoming more critical every day.

UPC and EDI technology

The universal product code (UPC) is a digital code that uniquely identifies an item of merchandise at the stock-keeping unit (SKU) level. This is most familiar in the form of a barcode, a series of vertical bars on an item or its packaging that computers can read. Today, perhaps 95 percent of *all* merchandise comes from the manufacturer with a barcode in place. If any of the merchandise in your store does not have one, you can easily assign one.

By using a scanner to record the UPC of every item you sell, you can have an extremely precise and accurate understanding of your daily sales. You can then implement a quick response (QR) strategy of immediately replenishing what you sell so that replacement items will be available to the next customers who want to buy them.

This goes hand in hand with the just in time (JIT) buying philosophy we described in Chapter 3. You buy just what you need and have it delivered just when you need it. JIT adds a whole new level of efficiency to a retail business: your inventory investment and risk are lower, while your customer service and ability to micromanage are higher.

If you then layer electronic data interchange (EDI) on top of this, you can be using essentially the same technology that the biggest and the best retailers in the world use to increase their efficiency.

EDI is the way that retailers and their suppliers share information electronically. It comprises a complete set of *forms* in a data format that is standard across all EDI packages, enabling a fast, efficient, and paperless transfer of information. Many suppliers today have web ordering systems that mimic full-blown EDI systems and that you can integrate with your merchandising software.

If you choose to embrace the rapid evolution of computer technology and use EDI, you will write purchase orders for your various suppliers electronically. At the end of the day, you will send them from your computer to either a third-party electronic mailbox or a web service through your Internet connection. The electronic mailbox or web service will then direct all of these purchase orders to the appropriate suppliers, who will pick them up from the electronic mailbox via their Internet connection the next morning.

As they process your orders, suppliers will send advance shipping notices and invoices through the electronic mailbox or web service. You will know exactly what merchandise you are getting long before it arrives, and you will need to scan just one barcode to enter every item in that shipment into your inventory when it does arrive. If you want, you can pay for the merchandise electronically as well.

Not many years ago, the technology behind UPC, QR, JIT, and EDI was available to only the largest retailers. Today, it is available to retailers of every size. We believe that before long, it will be a necessity.

Many retailers are already using EDI to communicate with their suppliers. This has enabled the suppliers to cut costs by reducing the number of people they employ to accept orders manually. If they once had six people handling mail and fax orders, they may now have just two. The trend is clear: Owner-operated retailers may soon have no choice but to use EDI and web-based ordering if they want to buy from those suppliers. As an alternative, some suppliers may charge more to retailers who cannot communicate with them electronically.

Because EDI and variations of it through the Internet are increasingly being used in retail technology, it will likely affect your business more than any other technology trend over the next few years. This means you should only buy a point of sale (POS) system if it either handles EDI directly or interfaces with web-based EDI vendor programs.

Once your system generates a purchase order, it is handy to be able to transmit that order to the vendor immediately and get a confirmation back right away.

The Internet

Many owner-operated retailers think that they should have their businesses on the Internet, but few can explain why. Media hype over the millions of people who have access to the Internet through their home and office computers has often blurred the true benefits.

To understand these benefits, you first need to understand that the Internet is by design chaotic. In keeping with its original national-defense purpose, messages move from computer to computer using roundabout routes that are prone to bottlenecks. This means that the Internet can at times be the electronic equivalent of a chaotic traffic jam involving millions of cars. And because companies and individual users are creating tens of thousands of pages on the Internet every *hour*, this traffic jam is growing exponentially.

Now imagine that you are sitting somewhere in the middle of this traffic jam and that you want someone on the outside to come and find your car among the millions of other cars. This illustrates just what it is like to have your business on the Internet. It is extremely difficult for a customer to find you, and it is getting more difficult every day.

Helping Google and other search engines find your website and then rank it highly *is* possible, however. You can learn how to optimize your site for search engines by contacting your local Internet service provider (ISP), almost all of whom have excellent help pages that will guide you through the process.

Because it has become such a universal way of sharing information, the Internet could well be a useful tool for your business. For example, you could use it to provide interest-specific information or detailed product knowledge to your current customers.

Directing your website primarily to current customers makes a lot of sense because these are the only people to whom you can realistically get your web address without advertising it widely. To make visiting your website worthwhile, customers should receive something more than they can get from you over the telephone. Perhaps you could post recipes if you operate a kitchenware store or videos from a Paris fashion show if you operate a womenswear store.

For many stores, providing information over the Internet is a much better business proposition than selling products over the Internet. That is because selling products over the Internet is very similar to being in the catalog business, and these two types of businesses are fundamentally different from operating a retail store. For example, catalog and Internet businesses have an average return rate of 20 percent, some of this being damaged merchandise that is not suitable for resale. This is a much higher return rate than any retail store has. If you also factor in the cost of shipping and warehousing, selling over the Internet can become quite an expensive proposition.

This does not, however, mean that you should totally ignore the opportunities that eBay offers owner-operated retailers. eBay has become a great place to clear old merchandise and avoid deep markdowns, and many retailers use it to help them move merchandise that their local customers have not bought.

It is relatively easy to set up a selling account on eBay, but we suggest that you do this using your own name instead of your store name. This will protect the brand image that your store has with local customers, and avoid any price confusion. Yahoo also offers the opportunity to set up an inexpensive storefront on its site.

The Internet makes it easy for customers to find you only if they are already looking for your store or for something very specific that you carry. Because there is no "foot traffic" on the web, people will need to see your website listed somewhere else — perhaps in a search engine such as Google — and then decide to get in touch.

When a potential customer does access your web page, he or she may run into some practical limitations:

- Not all computers download information from the web at DSL speed. A customer may be fine using a slower speed connection for a few pages of information or to look for something in particular, but not if he or she wants to browse through an entire 300-page catalog.

- You will have no control over the equipment that your customers use when visiting your website. A home page that looks great at one screen resolution or on one particular browser may look terrible at a different resolution or on another browser. You should test your site on the top three browsers and recognize that most customers today have screen resolution of at least 800 x 600, with the majority now at 1024 x 768 or better.

- Although web pages always take a certain amount of time to download and display in their entirety, customers may move on to another site if your page downloads too slowly. This can happen if you use a lot of pictures and Flash components. Customers are not interested in bells and whistles when they visit a website. Instead, they want useful information and they want it quickly. You need to test every page on your site for download speed.

As a professional retailer, you are neither an advertising specialist nor a technology specialist. For this reason, we suggest that you turn to outside professionals if you intend to set up a website for your business. You will find a huge number of Internet service providers listed in the Yellow Pages — as well as on the web itself. When choosing outside help, make sure that you choose someone who understands both advertising and technology.

Budgeting for Technology

Although we have referred to technology in almost all of the previous chapters, we thought we should wait until now to explain exactly what you need to buy and how much you should budget.

Your technology needs will include at least one personal computer equipped with some retail-specific hardware and software, plus some off-the-shelf software such as a spreadsheet program, a word processing program, and a desktop publishing program.

Retail-specific hardware should include the following:

- Cash drawer
- Protected standard keyboard or a specially manufactured cash register keyboard
- Credit card reader that is built into the keyboard
- Laser scanner that connects to the keyboard
- High-quality receipt printer
- High-speed modem or network card for credit card approval (a DSL line would be better)
- Tape backup system (CD/DVD is still not proven for long-term archival purposes)
- Uninterruptible power supply (UPS)
- Ticket printer
- Ink-jet or laser printer for reports and signs
- Debit card machine at POS for customers using debit cards

Retail-specific software should include the following:

- Point of sale (POS) program
- Merchandising (back office) program
- Customer database program
- Two or more of the above combined into an integrated package
- Accounting program

Most retailers invest between 1 percent and 2 percent of their annual net sales in technology. For owner-operated retailers just starting out, 3 percent would be a more realistic figure. This amount includes hardware, software, and training.

A good rule of thumb is that hardware and software should cost about 50 percent of the total amount you spend, leaving about 50 percent for training. Most retailers use a five-year depreciation period for their investment in technology, which is fine if you buy fairly close to the leading edge because you will not be left behind as quickly.

Here is an example of the way this investment breaks down:

do the calculation

Annual net sales		$800,000
x five years		$4,000,000
x 3%		$120,000
Total to spend with a five-year depreciation		$120,000
Hardware and software @ 50% of total		$60,000
Hardware @ 40%	$24,000	
Software @ 60%	$36,000	
Training @ 50% of total		$60,000

What will your investment in technology be?

Annual net sales		$_____
x five years		$_____
x 3%		$_____
Total to spend with a five-year depreciation		$_____
Hardware and software @ 50% of total		
Hardware @ 40%	$_____	
Software @ 60%	$_____	
Training @ 50% of total		$_____

Most owner-operated retailers can understand and accept the amount they should invest in hardware and software, but feel uncomfortable with the amount they should invest in training. This could be because they do not recognize that buying retail software is very different from buying off-the-shelf software.

In the case of retail software, you will probably need to use every feature the product offers to achieve your goal: running a profitable retail business. In the case of off-the-shelf software such as a word processing package, you will probably *not* need to use every feature the product offers to achieve your goal: for example, writing a letter.

Training will greatly lower the risks inherent in your investment in technology. These risks include your computer crashing when you have a lineup of customers, running out of an item because someone misread a report, and receiving the wrong item because someone did not scan a barcode properly.

If you do not allocate a full 50 percent of your investment in technology to training, we believe that you should allocate the same amount to losses due to these risks instead. You could be setting yourself up for a big financial loss if you miss out on the potential benefits that a point of sale (POS) system can provide because you do not understand how to use the various components properly.

a word to the wise

When you buy a POS system for your store or upgrade an existing system, you should arrange for training in a three-step process and document the specifics in a written agreement with your technology supplier.

The first step comes at the time of installation. The supplier should complete the installation, test that everything is working properly, and then walk your staff through the steps of recording a sale, accepting the various payment methods, making an even exchange, and so on.

The second step comes about 30 days after the installation. By then, your sales associates will have had a chance to practice and use the system in either simulated or actual transactions, and they will have any number of questions that they did not think to ask earlier. You, at the same time, will be getting ready to produce your first month-end reports.

The third, and most important, step comes three or four months after the installation. This is when the supplier returns to your store and shows you exactly how to profit from your investment in technology. You will learn to produce the specific reports you need and really understand the information your computer is providing.

Selecting the Right Integrated POS/Merchandising/CRM Package

If you wanted to, you could go out today and buy a simple POS-only program. This program would work as a cash register, recording sales and tracking SKUs — but it would not do anything else.

You could also buy a program that performs only merchandising or back-office functions such as writing purchase orders and looking after inventory control, accounts payable, and accounts receivable — but it would not do anything else.

Or you could buy just a customer database program. This would let you keep track of your customers by name, address, and telephone number — but it would not do anything else.

Finally, you could go out and buy an accounting program. This would provide accounting information such as your general ledger and your income statement — but it would not do anything else very easily.

Buying separate programs would mean a lot of work for you. You would have to write all sorts of "hooks" so that the programs could "talk" to each other. That is why retail-software suppliers sell integrated packages that incorporate the functions of three or four of their stand-alone programs.

We believe that the logical purchase for most owner-operated retailers today is an integrated POS, merchandising, and customer database package. Most integrated packages do not contain an accounting module. Instead, they simply export data to one of several accounting programs that have become standard in the industry. All you need to know is which one your integrated package exports to — and which one your accountant uses — so that you can buy it separately.

Accounting reports will not increase your business in any case. They provide historical information that will primarily interest your banker, your accountant, and the government. As a retailer, you need to worry much more about classification reports and customer database reports that you can use to increase sales and profitability today.

As you think through your business, it would be easy to wander off and spend a ridiculous amount of time learning about the huge number of technology alternatives available. Some of these relate to the basic "platform" or operating system that runs your computer. This *is* an important item because it will affect the speed and flexibility of your system, the number of upgrades you can expect to buy, and the number of other users you can call for guidance and support.

Without doubt, the world of retail software has shifted to the Windows® operating system — in part because it lets you do several things at the same time. For example, you can have a ticketing program producing price tickets while your back-office program is creating purchase orders and a sales associate is processing a sale.

And because it is a point-and-click computing environment, programs tend to be easy to learn and simple to use. Your POS, merchandising, and customer database programs will work in a way that is similar to your off-the-shelf word processing, spreadsheet, and desktop publishing programs.

Understanding the Many Things Your Integrated Package Should Do

The most common question that owner-operated retailers ask about technology is, "What is the best retail software to use?"

If there were a single right answer to give, we would probably give it — but there is not. Different stores will have somewhat different technology needs. We do, however, believe that any integrated package you buy should score well on the following "must have" checklist:

☐ *Adheres to the retail method of accounting.* It is easy to check this by asking your software supplier: "If I buy ten units at $5, another ten units at $6, and don't make any sales, what will the system show as the cost of these items?" If the answer is anything other than $5.50, the system does not use the retail method of accounting.

❏ *Easy to learn and use.* Over time, you will be training a number of new employees to use your POS system. You will want to get them up to speed quickly and efficiently, which means they should be able to handle the basics after 20 minutes and the rest of the system within a day or two.

❏ *Allows for fast checkout.* In today's retail world, this means having a scanner to read the UPC from every item in your store. There are several ways to process items that you cannot barcode directly — hardware stores do it all the time.

❏ *Accepts keystroke shortcuts in addition to both self-defined and supplier UPCs.* If you sell large quantities of a specific item, you can save significant time at the checkout by entering a one-digit keyboard shortcut instead of scanning the item.

❏ *Provides automatic credit card approval.* Rather than having a separate unit that clutters your cash and wrap, your POS system should let you simply swipe the customer's card and then look after getting the authorization and printing the necessary forms automatically.

❏ *Provides price lookup (PLU).* When you enter a keystroke shortcut or scan an item, you should see a brief description of the item and its price on your screen. This gives you some protection against data entry errors or customers switching price tickets.

❏ *Allows for suspended transactions.* Customers frequently leave their wallets in the car but do not notice until they get to a retailer's cash and wrap. If you have the ability to suspend a transaction while your customer goes to get his or her wallet, you will have fewer lineups and happier customers.

❏ *Handles foreign-currency transactions.* If tourists shop in your store, you will need to accept foreign currency and offer the current exchange rate. At a minimum, your POS system should accept foreign currency, calculate the exchange rate, calculate change in your own currency, and provide all relevant details on the receipt.

❏ *Accepts multiple tenders.* For whatever reason, a customer may want to pay for part of a purchase with a credit card, part with a check, and the rest with cash. Your POS system should let you handle this with a smile.

❏ *Looks up customers by telephone number as well as by name.* As you get into relationship marketing, you will want to link every transaction to a name in your database. If your memory is less than perfect, customers will forgive you for forgetting their telephone numbers, but not for forgetting their names.

❑ *Suggests related items as add-ons.* If you intend to follow our advice and focus your staff's attention on increasing the average transaction, you will certainly want this feature. If a sales associate scans a flashlight, for example, some of the better POS systems will automatically flash the word "batteries."

❑ *Looks up on-order items.* No matter how well you manage your inventory, you will sometimes run out of a certain item and face a customer who wants to know when you will be getting more. A good POS system will tell you what is on order and when it is scheduled to arrive.

❑ *Tracks special orders.* If you "special order" specific items for your customers, you should consider this feature a necessity. A good POS system will remind you about what is on special order and when it is due to arrive. You will keep customers who have placed special orders happier if you tell them about late deliveries instead of letting them tell you.

❑ *Comes with a 90-day money-back guarantee.* All of the off-the-shelf software sold in stores today comes with a 30-day money-back guarantee — and the price is much lower than the amount you will be investing in an integrated package. If a supplier is not prepared to offer a guarantee, you may want to consider how much confidence the supplier has in that software.

A checklist of these features, with room for notes, is included on the CD-ROM that accompanies this book.

We believe that the specific brand of computer system you buy is much less critical than being able to arrange local service. If something goes wrong, you will want to have someone nearby who can quickly get you operating again with a new keyboard, a new hard drive, or a new monitor. This local support could well come from your POS software supplier. In most cases, the company that sells you software will also be able to sell you hardware. Even if the hardware costs a bit more this way, there are many advantages to buying both from the same source.

that's a good idea

At the top of the list is a one-call repair service. You will never have to face a software supplier who blames a problem on your hardware supplier or a hardware supplier who blames a problem on your software supplier. You will appreciate the value of a single supplier the first time you have a problem on a busy Saturday afternoon.

The best advice we can offer about buying hardware is do not scrimp. It is not worth saving $250 on a receipt printer if it breaks down regularly. The same applies to your keyboard, your uninterruptible power supply, your tape backup, your telephone lines, and your modem.

Using Technology Wisely to Run a Profitable Business

The biggest difference between operating a store 35 years ago and operating one today is the amount of control and flexibility that an owner can have. The business is as much of an art as it has ever been, but technology now provides the solid foundation of science that retailers used to only dream about. By using current technology, you will be able to do the following:

1. Change the price of any item in your store whenever you wish and know exactly how much inventory you have at retail value and at cost at the end of each business day. This will help you protect things that are precious: your time and your assets.

2. Track every markdown by product code so that at the end of a season you will know your markdowns by supplier. Your negotiating position will be stronger if you can demonstrate that a given supplier represents 30 percent of your markdowns but only 15 percent of your sales.

3. Know your exact sales for every hour your store is open, how much each of your sales associates sells per hour or day, and your store's average transaction by hour, day, or week. All of these are important measures of productivity — and you will need to be *very* productive if you want to succeed in the retail business.

4. Look after reordering and purchase orders automatically. The more orders you write in your business, the more time you can save by letting a computer do most of the work. A good integrated package will drop the supplier's name and address into place, add your size and color grid, and even give you the details of the most recent purchase order you wrote to that supplier. Every hour you can save will be an hour you can spend serving customers.

5. Speed up your point of sale. No matter how long customers may take with their shopping, they hate lineups at the cash and wrap. Some people will put an item down and walk out of the store rather than wait. You cannot afford to have this happen in your business.

6. Run a maintained margin report for every classification in your store at the end of every month — and know immediately if you made or lost money, and why.

7. Keep a constant eye on your inventory. You will know what is selling and what is getting old. You will know when you are getting low on sizes or colors, and when you should reorder. You will know what merchandise to mark down and, once you take the markdown, how the lower price affects the rate of sale. This is far more information than you could possibly compile in your head.

8. Identify your 100 bestselling items by dollar volume for any period you wish. This can help you replenish the exact items that your customers are buying, making it much more likely that you can increase your sales.

9. Keep track of your customers. By knowing their names, addresses, and telephone numbers — not to mention all of the items they have ever bought in your store — you are demonstrating that your business is interested in more than a one-time transaction. If you are going to be successful, you must build long-term relationships with your customers.

10. Identify your 100 best customers by dollar volume and profit margin for any period that you wish. Your best customers should be absolute VIPs in your store, receiving regular communication from you and all sorts of special benefits and rewards.

a word to the wise

We have two rules to guide you as you consider the role that technology will play in your business:

- Rule 1: Technology must benefit the customer.
- Rule 2: If technology does not benefit the customer, do not use it.

The benefit of technology to the customer could take many forms. It could be a faster point of sale so that the customer spends less time waiting in line. It could be better operating efficiency so that you can lower the price the customer has to pay. It could be a better ability to relate to customers and understand their needs so that you can have the items on hand that they want to buy.

As a bonus, these benefits to the customer will also get you more business and save you some money.

The one thing that you should not do is get into technology for the sake of getting into technology. With no clear understanding of the ways that this investment will benefit the customer, you would be making a mistake.

Keeping Your Inventory, Sales, Profit, and Space in the Correct Balance

An additional way that technology can help you manage your business is through balance reports. When everything is working the way it should, your merchandise classifications will be in a logical balance. For example, if your widget classification represents 20 percent of your inventory, it will also represent 20 percent of your sales, 20 percent of your gross profit, and occupy 20 percent of your selling floor.

A good POS system will let you run reports showing your balance of inventory by classification, your balance of sales by classification, and your balance of margin by classification. You will have to measure your balance of selling floor the old-fashioned way: with a tape measure.

Once you have these figures, you may need to put on your merchant's hat to make allowances for the size and value of certain items in your inventory, since these could shift the percentages a few points in either direction. You then need to put on your bean counter's hat to decide, in the cold light of reality, if your widget classification is in a logical balance.

If it is in a logical balance, all is well. Otherwise, you will need to decide if you are carrying too much or too little inventory, applying a margin that is too high or too low, or perhaps giving the widgets too much or too little selling floor. You must relate these three to sales, of course, since your customers determined the sales by voting with their wallets, and you should never second-guess that information. We have included a "balance of business" calculator on the CD-ROM that accompanies this book.

Many owner-operated retailers today are not able to manage their businesses in this way because they did not set them up using technology in the first place. By starting from scratch in the age of technology, you can have a huge competitive advantage in the marketplace.

a word to the wise

Although we believe that you should use technology right from the start in your business, we admit that it will make your first year of operation more difficult than it would be otherwise. But the eventual payback makes this an absolute necessity.

An owner-operated retailer who is adding technology to an existing business should expect six months of challenges followed by four-and-a-half years of benefits, even with the best POS system. On top of these challenges, you will be facing all of the other challenges inherent in starting a business.

Your first year of operation will definitely not be easy. That is why we are painting a picture of where you want to go in your second year of operation.

Making an Informed Decision About POS Software Suppliers

As you look at specific POS software, we believe that you should look at the suppliers of those systems as well because you will be depending on both the software *and* the supplier. The company you choose to work with is going to become a very important partner in your business, one that can literally make or break your store. You need to understand two things in this regard.

First, although your POS supplier will become a partner in your business, he or she will not carry any of the responsibility for your decisions. You alone must do all of the research and planning that it will take to understand which software will work best for your business.

Second, you will always get what you pay for. If you choose to pay $3,600 rather than $36,000 for a software package, or $6,000 rather than $60,000 for post-installation training, you should expect that much in return but no more. As a retailer, you will often tell this to your customers. As a customer, you should understand what it means.

The $3,600 software package and the $6,000 training may be perfect for your business. The point is that only you can decide — and then carry the responsibility for your decision.

Questions for potential POS software suppliers

To ensure you make an informed decision about buying POS software for your store, we suggest that you contact at least three suppliers and ask them the following series of questions. We have included these on a blank form on the CD-ROM that accompanies this book so that you can make notes as you call.

(a) *How many retailers currently use your software?* It would be good to hear that several thousand other retailers have liked the software well enough to buy it. You certainly do not want to be one of a hundred. If the supplier has enough other customers who run businesses similar to yours, he or she will tend to design updates that meet your needs.

(b) *How many stores currently use your software?* The answer to this could be quite different from the answer to the previous question if some multilocation retailers have bought the software.

(c) *What are the names of ten current users I can contact?* You will know in advance that you are getting the names of satisfied customers only, but you do not need to worry about this now. The important thing is that you speak with other retailers who have hands-on experience with the software. You can always ask these contacts if they know of other users.

(d) *How long have you been in business? How many people do you employ?* If you find that the supplier set up shop a year ago and employs two people, you should question whether he or she will be able to provide the training and support you need — no matter how good the software is.

(e) *How many "releases" of this software have there been?* If you measure this against how long the supplier has been in business, you will have a good idea of how often the software is updated to provide the latest features. The average time between releases in the software industry is around 18 months.

(f) *How frequent and how extensive are your updates? What is the cost of these?* Many suppliers wrap their support and their updates together. For example, you might pay 15 percent of the original cost of the software to cover a year's technical support and any updates the supplier releases that year. If the supplier sells updates separately, find out how much these will cost.

(g) *Do I have a choice in buying updates?* You may already know the answer to this question, but if you do not, ask it now. Some suppliers require you to buy updates as a condition of buying the program initially because it is costly for them to support older versions of a program after they have released an update.

(h) *What kind of support can I get?* You need to understand how the supplier will support the software. Does the purchase price include support or will there be additional charges? Is this support by remote (i.e., using the Internet or a modem and phone line) or is it on-site? Is it available in the evenings and on weekends or just during regular business hours? Is there a toll-free number to call? The answers to these questions will vary from supplier to supplier; clearly, there are no right or wrong answers to any of these questions. What's important is that you understand what you are buying.

(i) *What is the minimum and optimum hardware configuration I need to run this software?* We said earlier that you should not scrimp on hardware. There are good reasons for buying the best you can afford. No matter what the supplier describes as a minimum hardware configuration, you should probably buy well above that. Think of this as an investment in the future of your business.

(j) *What hardware do most current users have?* If the answer is a particular brand name, you should consider buying that brand of computer. It will be much easier for the supplier's technical support people to help you if you have equipment that is familiar to them.

(k) *Do I have to use specific peripherals?* Some POS software will work properly only if you use a specific cash drawer, a specific scanner, or a specific printer. This is an issue only if you are not buying your hardware from the software supplier. You do not want to buy equipment that will not work with the total system.

(l) *Is this an integrated package?* Even if it is, you will probably have to buy a separate accounting package, as we explained earlier. However, you may also want to use word processing, spreadsheet, and desktop publishing programs in your business. You should ask up front which programs the POS software will and will not work with.

(m) *Can I buy only part of it now?* Most integrated packages are modular, which means you may be able to buy just one module to start. For example, you might want to buy just the POS module now and the merchandising module in six months.

(n) *Is there installation assistance?* If the answer is yes, how will it work? Will one of the supplier's engineers come to your store to install the program or will a third party handle the work on a contract basis? If so, how much direct experience does this third party have?

(o) *What, if any, additional software do I need?* If the supplier offers remote support — connecting the supplier's computer directly to your computer over a telephone line — you may need to buy a special modem or an additional software program to facilitate this. You may also need to buy networking software to connect the computers in your store if you have more than one.

(p) *How will this POS software pay for itself?* This is the "killer" question, the one that should separate the professional suppliers from the amateurs. If you hear an answer that approximately matches what we have told you in this chapter, you should be on solid ground. If the answer is wildly different, you will need to decide for yourself whom to believe.

a word to the wise

We will say this very clearly and plainly: You do *not* want a customized POS package.

Once they start to get an understanding of the POS package you think you need, some suppliers may propose a customized version of their regular software. *Do not buy it.*

First, you will pay more for customized software. Second, you will be out of the upgrade path and unable to purchase later versions of the software without again paying for customization. Third, the supplier's technical support people will not likely have your version of the software loaded on their machines when you call with a problem.

Modifications such as slight changes to the formatting of a report are usually easy and inexpensive, and you should have no problem with them. Customization, however, is a totally different proposition and may be very complicated to fine-tune. Perhaps you need to rethink your needs if 2,000 other retailers can use the standard version of the software while you cannot.

POS questions for retailers

To avoid making a mistake when buying POS software for your store, we suggest that you contact at least three users of the software and ask them the following questions. It does not really matter if these users are nearby or located in another city; most people will gladly answer your questions if you explain why you are calling and ask if they have time to speak with you.

Although it would be nice to speak with retailers who operate a store similar to yours, it is not crucial. The more important thing is to listen for answers from actual users that match closely with those given by the supplier. We have included the following questions on a blank form on the CD-ROM that accompanies this book so that you can make notes as you call.

(a) *How long have you had the package?* If the user has had the package for less than a year, you may hear some negative comments. If the user has had the package for less than six months, you will *probably* hear some negative comments. This is because most users need to go through a full annual cycle before they become truly comfortable with a POS package.

(b) *Do you use the complete package or just one or two of the modules?* Although the supplier has listed this retailer as a user of their software, the store may be using only part of the package. To get a true comparison, you need to speak with users who have experience with everything that you are intending to buy and use.

(c) *Which release are you using?* Asking this question will enable you to compare apples to apples. If the retailer you speak with is using version 2.0 and you are intending to buy version 4.0, you need to understand that his or her experience may not hold true for you.

(d) *What do you like best about the software?* This open-ended question will let the user say whatever positive things he or she likes about the supplier's product. You may find some of the comments quite encouraging.

(e) *What is the biggest problem, if any, that you have had with the software?* This provides an opportunity for a user to give you his or her view of the downside of the supplier's product. If you hear of a problem, you should ask additional questions to help you understand the situation. When did this problem start? Was it a software problem or a hardware problem? How did the user solve the problem?

(f) *What hardware do you have?* If the software is not performing well, the retailer's hardware may not be powerful enough to run it. If you buy fairly close to the leading edge of technology, including ample RAM and storage, you may not have the same problem.

(g) *How would you rate the supplier's support?* This question should help you determine whether the software supplier will go the extra mile to provide good customer service. You will care greatly about this issue the first time you have a problem. If you hear great things about the software but not-so-great things about the support, you should probably elect not to buy from that supplier.

(h) *Do you know of any other users I could contact?* This question may help you find users of the software who may not be the supplier's satisfied customers. Do not worry too much if you cannot locate additional users, since the answers you would get from most users would be surprisingly consistent.

(i) *Would you buy this software again?* This question cuts right to the bottom line. If a user says he or she would not buy the software again, we believe that you should talk to quite a few other users who *would* before you decide to buy the software.

---

that's a good idea

Consider using a notebook computer as your back-office machine. Among other things, this will help you enjoy some sort of a family life. When the store closes, you can simply unplug your notebook from the network and head home. Then, after the kids are in bed, you can flip open the machine and complete work that you were not able to do during the day.

If your notebook has a network connection, you can use your home DSL line to connect to the store computer to get the latest sales figures or inventory counts at any hour of the day. This will be especially handy if you are out of town on a buying trip and need to know the sales of a particular item for last week or last month.

put it to work

We suggest that you pause here to look back over the topics we have covered in this chapter on technology. While everything is fresh in your mind, you need to decide how well prepared you are for this part of an owner-operated retailer's job.

You then need to decide what three technology issues you can work on immediately, what three pieces of additional information you need, and which three people you should telephone or meet with soon.

How well prepared are you for technology? (Circle one.)

READINESS		RATING
Need to hire a consultant	✐	1
Need to take some courses	✐	2
Need to read some books	✐	3
Can handle this with effort	✐	4
Can handle this in my sleep	✐	5

What three technology issues can you work on immediately, and what can you do about each of them?

1_____

2_____

3_____

What three pieces of additional information do you need to better understand the technology part of your job?

1_____

2_____

3_____

Which three people should you telephone or meet with soon about the technology part of your job?

1_____

2_____

3_____

Please transfer these answers to the Action Plan in Appendix 1.

7
CUSTOMER SERVICE

This part of your job includes:

- Operating like an old-time retailer in terms of knowing your customers

- Competing with vending-machine retailers by adding significant value

- Creating top-of-mind customer awareness by what happens within your four walls

- Providing extra-mile service that will truly amaze your customers

- Looking at your business and providing what customers say they want

- Offering a make-it-right refund policy and assuming returns are "righteous"

- Implementing relationship marketing and one-to-one communication

- Identifying your 100 or 200 best customers and creating a VIP club

your job description

Knowing Your Customers

We believe that you will be successful in retail if you focus your business on two principles: customer service that goes the extra mile and the one-to-one communication with customers known as *relationship marketing*.

The former is the best way to make your business stand out from the crowd; the latter is the best way to keep it there. Both are important aspects of providing first-rate customer service — a challenge that North American retailers have grappled with for years.

In several important ways, however, an owner-operated retailer faces challenges today that are quite different from the ones that an old-time retailer faced. A century ago, you would have had a store on Main Street in your city or town, held a position of trust and respect in the community, and personally known all of the customers you served in the store. You would have known their names, where they lived, how many children they had, and what they did for a living. You would also have remembered all of the items they had ever purchased in your store.

It would have been relatively easy to know your customers because you would have lived in the same community, walked on the same sidewalks each day, and attended the same church on Sundays.

Today, a more likely scenario is that Main Street is empty, customers vaguely distrust you, and you know almost none of them by name.

We believe that as a retailer today, you need to get "back to the future" in terms of knowing your customers, and structure your business as if *these* were the good old days. In other words, the business you operate in the early part of the 21st century should look much like the business you would have operated in the early part of the 20th century — picture Main Street U.S.A. in Disneyland, if you are not familiar with the era.

Structuring your business this way will help you offset three important trends that have increased the competition for customers in recent years:

1. Developers and retailers for many years built stores at a much faster rate than was warranted by our population increase. About 100 percent more stores are now trying to sell to about 15 percent more people.

2. Retailers have created some very successful new formats. "Category killers" and big-box retailers are now taking business away from

specialty stores the way specialty stores once took business away from department stores. Many of the biggest retailers are getting even bigger while many of the smallest retailers, those who are unprepared, are falling by the wayside.

3. The customer profile is changing. You no doubt know that baby boomers make up the largest generation in the history of North America. By virtue of sheer numbers, these people are a significant force in the economy as they move through the various stages of life.

   Baby boomers are now moving out of their peak purchasing years and shifting their purchasing patterns. They do not need many more homes, cars, televisions, or clothes — and most have given up competitive sports in favor of hiking. This, however, is happening at the same time as their children graduate from college and leave home — which means that, with years to go before retirement, a lot of baby boomers have a newly found disposable income to spend on luxuries and life experiences. They remember customer service the way it used to be, and they consider it important.

   In contrast, the children of the baby boomers are just reaching the stage of life during which people buy a lot of possessions. As their parents did before them, they will buy homes, cars, televisions, clothes, and tennis-club memberships. But their expectations of service will be quite different. We will talk more about this in Chapter 8.

Most experts predict that all three of these trends will continue well into the future, which means that retail will probably never see another purchasing binge like the one in the 1970s and 1980s that was caused by the baby boom. Instead, retailing will get more and more competitive.

If you believe that "most experts" are correct in their predictions, the direction you must take in your retail business becomes clear. You will need to work hard for each sale and give your customers significant reasons why they should shop with you. This is exactly what extra-mile service and relationship marketing will help you do.

You will *exceed* your customers' expectations by doing all the little things well that most retailers do not do at all: giving more to your customers for less, which will require you to keep your expenses under control while you "wow" them with your service. Not an easy task!

**that's a
good idea**

One great way that you can learn more about your customers is to provide comment cards.

Two groups of customers tend to use comment cards: those you have made very angry and those you have made very happy. This means that using comment cards for research is most useful for damage control and for getting ideas from people who really like your store. Comment cards are *not* very useful for getting the opinions of a good cross section of your customers.

To help you design an effective customer comment card, we suggest that you spend time in the coming weeks collecting customer comment cards from every business you visit. Do not restrict yourself just to retail stores — grab one every chance you get. After a month or so, sit down with your collection and review each one from the perspective of a customer.

Based on our own research, here are some of the things we like to see on a comment card:

- The question: "How did we do today?" in big, bold letters.
- Prepaid postage so that the customer can return it by mail to the store's owner instead of handing it to a sales associate.
- The opportunity to rate efficiency, friendliness, accuracy, knowledge, quality, value, prices, selection, cleanliness, and overall satisfaction.
- A five-point rating scale ranging from below average to remarkable, with average in the middle.
- A design that is easy to read and not too crowded, with well-spaced lines for the customer's written comments.
- Space to provide a name, address, and telephone number if the customer chooses.
- The name of the person who will be reading the card and a check box that allows the customer to indicate whether he or she is agreeable to being contacted for follow-up.
- The words: "Thank you for your comments."

Competing with Vending-Machine Retailers by Adding Significant Value

From the perspective of a customer, shopping at one of the big-box retailers is very similar to shopping at a vending machine. Neither asks what you want because they expect you to know that when you arrive, and both reduce the shopping experience to its simplest terms. As a customer, you walk in, put your money in the slot, pull the lever, and wait as a product slides down the chute.

Vending machines are both very efficient and very profitable for their owners, but they have one big drawback from a customer's perspective: they will happily sell "landfill." We use this term to describe any item a customer buys that does not meet his or her needs.

Think for a moment about your own home. Somewhere in your basement, garage, closet, bathroom, or kitchen you probably have at least one thing that you bought but never used. It might be a tool, a can of paint, a sweater, or some skin cream, but we will bet you have something.

You may not think of this item as landfill just yet, but deep in your heart, you already know. That item will sit in your basement, garage, closet, bathroom, or kitchen until you sell it in a yard sale, give it away, or send it with the rest of the trash to a landfill site.

Now think about where you bought this item. The odds are good that you bought it from a vending machine — a retailer who metaphorically invited you to walk in, put your money in the slot, pull the lever, and wait as a product slid down the chute.

This retailer did not care the least bit about you as a person or your needs. He or she probably sold you the item at a low, low price, but that did not leave the retailer with enough money to provide a professional sales associate who could answer your questions and help you understand what you needed to buy. Instead, you bought landfill.

As you develop your retail business, you should regularly ask yourself this question: "What is the difference between what I am doing and what a vending machine does?" If the answer is nothing, you are in deep trouble. A vending-machine retailer can simply undercut your prices and put you out of business.

To prevent this, you need to add value to every transaction. One of the best ways to do this is to provide extra-mile service and always take the time to understand your customers' needs. This is something that you can do well but a vending-machine retailer cannot do at all.

If you can figure out what it would take to make your customers' purchases complete and wonderful, and then find ways of doing that, you stand a good chance of lasting in the retail business. You could start by refusing to sell landfill, perhaps making this principle into a slogan:

> Our store is not going to let you buy useless stuff. Instead, we will provide you with all kinds of complete and wonderful solutions to your needs.

Not every customer will respond to this. Perhaps 20 percent of all customers shop on price alone and are quite happy to do their shopping at a vending machine. They do not care about pretty stores, and they are not interested in what some retailers think of as service.

You would be making a big mistake if you tried to build your business on this group because you will never be able to build relationships with customers who make purchases based on price alone. Those people will always go down the street to save a dime and around the corner to save a quarter.

This does not imply that the remaining 80 percent of shoppers do not care about price. On the contrary, these people care very much about what they pay in relation to what they receive. In other words, they care about value. They will expect you to justify your price, to explain *why* an item is worth the amount you are asking for it. Said another way, price will be an issue only in the absence of value.

We believe that you can probably charge 20 percent more than the lowest price in the market on a given item *if* you deliver at least *double* the difference in value. If you do not provide value and an explanation of the concept of value, your business will not succeed.

If you decided to adopt the slogan we proposed earlier, you may now want to add another sentence:

> We will not let any customer leave the store until he or she has the full benefit of our knowledge.

This slogan alone will set you apart from the vending-machine retailers. However, you will then have to tackle the difficult part: You will have to "walk the walk" and actually provide that extra-mile service.

We know of a building supply retailer who had to explain the concept of value to one of his customers, and he did it very well.

A customer rushed into the store one day and asked this retailer if he had any 4' x 8' sheets of good-one-side plywood. The retailer said that he did. The customer, a contractor in the middle of building a house, then asked how much the plywood cost. The retailer replied that it was $19.95 a sheet.

The customer responded that the same plywood was only $17.95 a sheet at a competing store down the street. The retailer then asked the rather obvious question: "Why not buy it there?"

"Because it's out of stock," said the contractor. To which the retailer replied, "When we are out of stock, *our* price is $15.95 a sheet."

He then went on to explain that his store had plywood that day because he made it a policy to stock sufficient inventory at all times. "We don't want to inconvenience you by not having the product you want, when you want it," he said. He also explained that his store employed only knowledgeable, friendly sales associates who could answer virtually any question and would gladly help load purchases onto the customer's truck.

"All of this costs money," the retailer explained. "And although we may be a bit more expensive on some items occasionally, we believe that the level of service we provide will more than make up the difference."

With some tongue-in-cheek humor, he explained the value that his store delivered, in this case to a contractor who was paying carpenters much more than the equivalent of $2 a sheet to do nothing until the plywood arrived. The contractor bought 24 sheets that day and has been back many times since.

Creating Top-of-Mind Customer Awareness

One of your biggest challenges as an owner-operated retailer will be to create top-of-mind awareness. This means that when a customer thinks of your product or service, he or she will immediately think of your store. To understand this point, try the following test: What is the first product you think of when we say "laundry detergent"?

The brand name of one particular laundry detergent immediately pops into most people's minds. There is a good reason for this. The manufacturer has spent many millions of advertising dollars imprinting this brand name on our brains over the years. It has created top-of-mind awareness. Your challenge is to do the same thing in your business with your target customers, but without spending the many millions of advertising dollars.

You will create a certain amount of awareness through advertising, but you will mostly create it through what happens within your own four walls. If your customers have a mediocre in-store experience, they may not even bother to memorize your store name. However, if your customers have an unpleasant in-store experience, they *will* remember both your name and the bad experience they had.

Here is some first-hand customer experience research to do: Go into any shopping mall and take a seat where you can watch customers coming out of a particular store for about 30 minutes. Take along a pen and a copy of Worksheet 3 to record your observations. (The scorecard is also on the CD-ROM.)

As each customer leaves the store, decide if that person looks thrilled and happy, bored and distant, or agitated and angry. Record that observation on the following scorecard. At the end of 30 minutes, move down the mall to watch customers coming out of another store.

Repeat the process until you have recorded observations at four stores and then stop to calculate totals for the session. You will have some great information about the ways that customers react to stores. Based on your observations, what percentage of the customers had a mediocre shopping experience and may not even remember the name of the store at which they were shopping?

WORKSHEET 3
CUSTOMER EXPERIENCE SCORECARD

	Thrilled and happy	Bored and distant	Agitated and angry
Store 1			
Store 2			
Store 3			
Store 4			
Total customers in each category			
Total customers you observed today			
Percentage	_____ %	_____ %	_____ %

The rewards of customer loyalty are worth a large expenditure of effort if you consider the lifetime value of a customer to your business.

Grocery shopping is a familiar situation, so let's calculate your lifetime value to the local supermarket. We will assume that you shop every week for a family of four, which means you probably spend about $200 each week on groceries. Over the course of a year, we can conclude that you spend about $10,400 in the supermarket.

Now let us assume that you will shop in that same supermarket for ten years before you sell your home and move elsewhere. This means that you will have spent $104,000 on groceries during your time as a customer in that supermarket.

Consider this for a minute. People who give away checks for $50,000 often get their picture in the newspaper, and yet here you are, walking the supermarket aisles every week with an even larger check in your hand. Shouldn't you at least get your picture in the store's newsletter?

Do the people in that supermarket even know your name? Do they ever say thank you? Should you expect a farewell card when you move? How long will it take them to notice that you are gone?

Providing Extra-Mile Service

We often speak to retailers about the importance of "going the extra mile." By this we mean providing extra-mile service — doing things that will truly amaze your customers. Many of these will be both simple and inexpensive, and yet few of your competitors will bother to make the effort. You will find that there is very little traffic on the extra mile.

Here is a challenge. Think back over the last six months and come up with one good example of extra-mile service that you have personally experienced as a customer in a retail store. This should be something that truly amazed you, something so good that it *still* stands out in your mind.

A participant in one of our workshops came up with a great example: When someone broke into her car, stole the radio, and did extensive damage, she found herself getting the runaround from The Big Insurance Corporation. It would not cover all of the legitimate repairs, meaning that, far beyond the amount of her deductible, being the victim of a crime was going to cost her a lot of money.

Then she met an owner-operated retailer who, unlike The Big Insurance Corporation, treated her as a valued customer. The people at this store provided extra-mile service, and they did it several times.

When she dropped off her car to have a new radio installed, a staff person drove her all the way across town so she could get to work on time. The store then did the installation, called her when it was finished, and offered to come to pick her up.

The biggest surprise came when she saw the bill. The store had given her the radio, which she was paying for personally, at cost. They had also replaced the wires on her car alarm, which the thief had cut but The Big Insurance Corporation refused to cover, and fixed some related damage. There was no charge on the bill for this additional work.

When she asked the owner-operated retailer why, he replied that when his car had been broken into four years earlier, The Big Insurance Corporation *had* paid for replacing the wires on his car alarm and fixing some related damage. When she had brought her car in, the retailer found his supporting documentation and said that he would send it to the insurance company along with an invoice for the work not covered.

Our workshop participant was amazed. That day, she told 125 people about her good experience with the store. She very likely told other people about it as well, because that is how word-of-mouth advertising works.

Two years later, we took time to visit the business she had described, and we found an owner-operated retailer who was thriving.

To create this kind of "apostle" for your business, you will have to judge the extra-mile service you provide from the perspective of your customers. If 80 percent of your customers expect you to do something and you do not do it, you are not going the extra mile. If 80 percent of your customers expect you to do something and you do it, you are still not going the extra mile.

Only when 80 percent of your customers do *not* expect you to do something and you do it will you be going the extra mile. You will know you are succeeding when customers react to your extra-mile service with words such as, "Wow, that's amazing. I've never heard of a store doing that before." Even then, you will be earning customer trust and loyalty just one small step at a time.

The good news is that as you earn customer trust and loyalty, not to mention a reputation for providing excellent service, customers will *expect* you to go the extra mile for them. This is a wonderful position to be in, because it will push you to find even more ways to meet and exceed those expectations.

The bad news is that out of 100 customers for whom you go the extra mile, perhaps 20 will not even notice. The majority of people, perhaps 60, will notice. Some of them may say thank you. If you are lucky, they may even remember the name of your store and come back sometime in the next three months.

That leaves perhaps 20 customers who will notice, say thank you, remember the name of your store, come back sometime in the next three months, and may even tell other people about your extra-mile service. You can build a very profitable retail business if you satisfy the needs of these customers.

Giving Customers What They Want

Looking at your business from your customers' perspective can be a fascinating experience. Things often look very different from the other side of the counter. Here are the results of some recent research that identified the top six things customers look for when they shop. As an owner-operated retailer who cannot compete with category killers and big-box retailers on price, you will be happy to see that price was at the bottom of the list.

1. *Convenience.* Given all of the stresses of their fast-paced lives, customers want shopping to be fast and easy. They will appreciate anything you do to help make it so. For example, you could offer delivery to anywhere in the world. You would not have to offer it free; you would just have to offer it. To a customer who needs to get a birthday gift to Sydney, Australia, by the weekend, you will be providing extra-mile service that he or she will gladly pay for.

2. *Selection.* You can have a beautiful store and wonderful staff, but if you do not have the products your customers want, they cannot buy from you. Many category-killer stores have built their businesses around having the best selection, not necessarily the lowest prices.

   As an owner-operated retailer, you will deal personally with your customers day after day. If you listen carefully to what they tell you, you should be able to offer an assortment and selection of merchandise that is almost perfect for them.

3. *Peace of mind.* Most customers want reassurance that they are buying the right item and that you will help them if they have any problems. One of the best things you can say to a customer is, "You cannot make a mistake when buying in my store." This is where understanding lifetime value becomes an advantage. If an item is not right, you are going to make it right instead of worrying about making or losing money on that particular sale. You know that in the long run you will make significant money from that customer.

4. *Product knowledge.* We said earlier that you can charge more than the lowest price in the market only if you deliver at least double the difference in value. One way to do that is to have friendly and approachable sales associates who know a great deal about the items they sell — and know how to research anything that they do not know.

   One thing sales associates should avoid, however, is using jargon. In most product classifications, experts use certain words to talk about how an item performs or what its components are. You should never assume that anyone else knows the meaning of your specialized words. Jargon intimidates more customers than it impresses. And remember, once the customer knows more about a product than your staff, you are in big trouble. Invest in product knowledge for your staff.

5. *Total service.* This phrase implies more than just having a friendly, approachable, and knowledgeable staff. Among other things, it implies: having a complete assortment of merchandise on hand so that customers do not waste trips; displaying merchandise so that customers can find it; and providing appropriate lighting so that customers can see colors and read price tags easily.

   There are many great books about customer service in any bookstore or library. As you build your retail business, we believe that you should buy an armload of these books and spend a lot of time reading about businesses that deliver it well — and then share the books with all of your sales associates.

6. *Price.* Most customers are looking for a fair price, which is not the same thing as the lowest price in the market. You probably understand this intuitively from your own experience. Nobody wants to feel cheated. It is rare that we ever question the price of something that has performed above and beyond our expectations; it is often when something breaks or does not work well that we feel cheated on price.

Identifying extra-mile service opportunities

The participants at one of our workshops developed an impressive list of things they could do to provide extra-mile service for their customers. Their suggestions appear on Worksheet 4. To help you see how a retail business looks from the other side of the counter, take a few minutes to compare the list of extra-mile service opportunities with the six things that customers look for when they shop. Beside each opportunity, mark whether it meets the customers' desire for convenience, selection, peace of mind, product knowledge, total service, or price. We have included a blank copy of the extra-mile service form on the CD-ROM that accompanies this book.

a word to the wise

A study published originally in the *Harvard Business Review* provides a fascinating look at the issue of customer loyalty. Researchers asked customers to rate their satisfaction with stores on a scale of one to five, where one was extremely dissatisfied and five was very satisfied. They also asked about the likelihood of the customers shopping at those stores again.

The findings were —

- Customers who reported that they were not extremely dissatisfied but less than satisfied had an average likelihood of shopping at the store again of about 20 percent.

- Customers who reported that they were more than satisfied but less than very satisfied had an average likelihood of shopping at the store again of about 50 percent.

- Customers who said they were very satisfied had an average likelihood of shopping at the store again of about 90 percent.

	1	2	3	4	5
	Extremely dissatisfied	Somewhat dissatisfied	Slightly dissatisfied	Satisfied	Very Satisfied
Likelihood of shopping again		20%		50%	90%

The conclusion: only when you have customers who are very satisfied will you have a better-than-even chance of getting them back into your store.

WORKSHEET 4
EVALUATING EXTRA-MILE SERVICE

	Convenience	Selection	Peace of mind	Product knowledge	Total service	Price
Producing an electronic customer newsletter that contains product information but no sales pitch, sent by email only to people who want to receive it.						
Offering a phone-ahead or online ordering system that lets the store prepare a customer's order and have it ready for fast pickup.						
Providing tourist maps and change for an exact-fare bus system in a downtown tourist area.						
Adopting batteries-included pricing in a toy store.						
Providing a toll-free telephone number in a store that has a lot of out-of-town customers.						
Staying open for a customer who arrives close to closing time until that customer has completed his or her shopping						
Free delivery and installation in an art-framing store.						
Repairing or arranging for local repairs to items that a customer would otherwise have to return to the manufacturer — a process that can take many weeks.						
Phoning around to area schools to get the school-supply lists that harried parents may not have when doing their back-to-school shopping.						
Providing unlimited in-home technical support at no charge for computer purchasers.						
Delivering clothing purchases to customers' homes when the free-of-charge alterations are complete.						
Providing links on the store's website to good sources of "neutral" information about the main products it sells, and an in-store computer on which to access it.						

Offering a Make-It-Right Refund Policy

Your store's refund policy is an excellent opportunity to provide extra-mile service for your customers. As a retailer who understands the lifetime value of a customer, there is really only one refund policy you can have: "If something is wrong, we will make it right."

The fastest way to kill your reputation as an extra-mile retailer is to post a sign behind the cash register that says, "No cash refunds." When we see a sign like this, it is almost always in a store where the owner feels he or she has been ripped off by one too many unscrupulous customers who purchased an item, used it or wore it, and then returned it the next day for a refund.

This certainly does happen, but not often enough compared with the number of transactions a store has in total to make it worth punishing every other customer for the deception of a few. When you look at the big picture, surprisingly few customers ever use a store's refund policy.

It is easy to follow a make-it-right policy when you are dealing with a wonderful customer who comes in regularly, pays full price, never questions your word, and almost never complains. You are happy to do whatever it takes to make it right.

The difficult time comes when you are dealing with an angry customer who comes in twice a year, never pays full price, always questions your word, and usually complains. It is tough to make it right under those circumstances, but you must, to a point.

In both cases, you should assume that this return is a righteous return. You should assume that somehow you sold a damaged, defective, or unsatisfactory product. In other words, you made a mistake, and the problem is yours.

What should you do? Walk toward the customer and apologize. This is only polite, and it may help calm an angry customer. Next, you ask the obvious question: "What's wrong?" Listen carefully to what the customer says and ask questions to make sure that you understand the problem fully.

Then you should apologize again and validate the quality of your store: "I'm sorry. This should not have happened. We take pride in selling top-quality merchandise and offering first-quality service. How can I make it right for you?"

The customer may want a replacement item (be certain that *it* works) or he or she may want a refund. In the end, most customers want very little beyond what they have already paid for. This is when you can really provide extra-mile service. Give the person what he or she wants and even a little more.

If the customer wants a replacement item, giving him or her more might mean offering the next model up at no additional charge. If he or she wants a cash refund, it might mean giving the customer the money back and a gift certificate as well. By giving something extra, you are making up for the time and the aggravation that your mistake cost the customer.

If you respect and value your customers, you need to *prove* it through the things that happen within your own four walls. You might want to develop a mission statement that says something like this:

> We are a small owner-operated retailer, deeply committed to satisfying our customers' needs and wants. We are in this business for the long term, and we therefore believe in total customer satisfaction.

An important part of providing extra-mile service for your customers is ensuring that each of your sales associates has the same decision-making authority that you have when it comes to making exchanges and refunds. Having a make-it-right refund policy means little if everyone has to check with you before making what should be an obvious decision.

Having said that, we also believe that you should protect yourself from the few customers who will abuse your make-it-right refund policy if you let them. If a customer wants to make what you consider a less than righteous return, you should give the refund but make note of the incident in a "preferred customer" book that you keep by the cash register.

If you get three less-than-righteous returns from the same customer in a given period — six months, perhaps — you are fully justified in declining the third request.

When a customer shops in your store, you will no doubt try to make the entire transaction as smooth and enjoyable as possible. But what will you do at the end of the sale? What kind of a message will you give that customer as he or she is leaving?

The following are two very different messages that we have taken from real-life retailers. As a customer, which one would you prefer?

Store A:

On the back of the sales associate's business card:

Thank you for shopping at (store name). I have enjoyed assisting you and I want you to know that I personally guarantee your satisfaction. If you have any problem or question, please call me and I will make it right. Thank you again. (Sales associate's signature)

Store B:

On the back of the cash register receipt in small type:

At (store name), we work very hard to provide you with product knowledge on the nature and value of everything we sell. We will gladly accept a return of merchandise within 30 days with proof of purchase (our cash register receipt) for exchange or credit. Goods can be returned for reasons of defect or dissatisfaction but we exclude accidental damage and tampering. At Christmas, out of consideration to the season, we extend the facility until January 31st. At this time of year we waive proof of purchase for readily identifiable goods but will input the lowest sale price for exchange or credit purposes. No cash refunds are possible. This includes credit refunds to credit cards. This is in conformity with independent industry standards and frankly is necessary if we are to remain in business. Within the boundaries of this policy, the staff is encouraged to seek your satisfaction. Currently we charge a minimum of $7.50 for all services and repair work (silver from $12.00 and up) sent out of the store. Please inquire about our extensive repair services for sterling silver and fashion jewelry. Plated items do react differently with individual customers and therefore we cannot be held responsible. Please avoid applying perfume or hair spray near any jewelry. Other warranties may apply. For further inquiries, call head office at (telephone number).

Implementing Relationship Marketing and One-to-One Communication

When your extra-mile service is fully in place, you can shift your attention to relationship marketing: targeted one-to-one communication with your customers.

Relationship marketing does not replace one-to-many communication. For generating new customers, there is still an important role for newspaper ads, flyers, and radio commercials to play in your business. We suggest only that you set aside part of your total communication budget for the personal connection that we believe you should have with each of your existing, loyal customers.

To help you understand what this personal connection might be, we offer four real-life examples of relationship marketing programs. These come from owner-operated retailers whom we know and respect. Each demonstrates a different level of connection with customers.

Relationship marketing level 1

- Has a mailing list of 23,000 names compiled over the last 12 years. Keeps the mailing list current by having the post office return undelivered mail, which adds to the cost.

- Provides comment cards that allow customers to send feedback, via postage prepaid.

- Has incentives that encourage sales associates to ask customers if they want to be on the mailing list, but customers complete the actual enrollment form.

- Mails to customers twice each season: first a regular-price, full-color catalog and later an end-of-season promotional piece. This second mailing includes a motivator that says, "Please bring in this card to receive your discount." By keeping track, the store identifies which customers buy generally during sales.

Relationship marketing level 2

- Has a loyalty program called the Corporate Club that customers "join" automatically once they spend $3,000 a year.

- Offers Corporate Club customers additional services such as free alterations, shopping by appointment, personal fashion consultations, fashion shows and seminars, advance notice of sales, and free delivery within a specified area.

- Uses client books in which sales associates track purchases made by their personal customers. Sales associates also keep notes on a customer's color preferences, size, birthday, and any relevant career or family information.

- Aims to contact each Corporate Club member eight times a year through telephone calls, personal emails, thank-you cards, and other personal touches, but places the full responsibility for building Corporate Club relationships in the hands of sales associates.

- Sends a gift to the store's very best customers each Christmas to thank them for their business.

Relationship marketing level 3

- Demonstrates that the store cares about its customers by filling the wall behind the cash and wrap with photos and postcards from the store's young customers.

- Employs sales associates who must really enjoy their jobs because they are always smiling.

- Gave up mailings and flyers three seasons ago and started to call customers on the telephone. Now hires university students to call all 5,000 customers in the database. Callers do not try to sell anything; they just let customers know about something new in the store. Twenty percent of these customers come into the store.

- Has a loyalty program called the Bonus Club that gives customers a $30 gift certificate when they reach $300 in purchases.

- Uses technology to link every transaction to a customer name, address, and telephone number. The store can identify which customers bought a given item so that staff can call those customers when a coordinating, matching, or complementary item arrives. Fifty percent of customers contacted come into the store.

Relationship marketing level 4

- Provides each sales associate with a list of his or her customers who spent more than $200 in the last two weeks, including a breakdown of the items that each customer bought. The sales associates then call their customers to ask one question: "Is everything satisfactory?"

- Uses database queries to target promotional mailings to very small groups of customers. For example, if a shipment of expensive bathrobes arrives, sales associates may write personal letters to the 20 or 30 customers who purchased a pair of silk pajamas but not a bathrobe during the past 12 months.

- Ties new items to specific customer profiles. When considering whether to stock a line of very expensive dress slacks, for example, the manager might buy a small number and then personally phone his or her best dress-slack customers and ask them to try the item and relate their comments.

- Adds an additional personal touch by having sales associates write a brief note on every form letter they send. This little extra adds an additional 25 percent to the response rate.

a word to the wise

Relationship marketing offers your business savings in four important areas — savings that go straight to the bottom line:

- You can reach customers much less expensively by mail than you can through advertising in the traditional media. Email is even cheaper, but it has become so common and associated with spam in some customers' minds that these customers may respond better to postal mail.

- Your sales associates spend much less time with good customers because they already know so much about them. This saves significant time determining customers' needs.

- Good customers are more forgiving of errors and they return less merchandise.

- You make higher margins from your good customers because they do not nickel-and-dime you every time they visit the store.

Identifying Your Best Customers and Creating a VIP Club

It may take you an entire year to set up a relationship marketing program. The most important things you need to do during that year are to identify your 100 or 200 best customers by dollar volume and then design rewards or incentives so that *these* customers will benefit most from them.

You need to create your relationship marketing database knowing how you will eventually use it. At a minimum, we believe that you will want to run the big three queries: frequency, recency, and amount.

The frequency query tells you how often each of your customers shops in your store. One may buy from you every second week, while another may buy from you only once or twice a season. There is a big difference between the importance to your business of these two customers.

The recency query tells you when each of your customers last shopped in your store. One may have shopped only two weeks ago and will have seen all of the latest merchandise, while another may not have shopped yet this season. You will say very different things to these two customers when you call them.

The amount query tells you how much each of your customers spent in your store during whatever period you choose to examine.

Although many owner-operated retailers think first of the POS and merchandising functions of an integrated retail software package, the customer relationship management (CRM) or database function is every bit as important.

For example, a computerized database would let you find the name, address, and phone number of every customer who used to spend at least $200 in your store once a month but who has not shopped there for the past three months. Once you know who these people are, you can call them personally to ask why — or send them a "Come back soon" letter and an incentive to do so.

To understand how powerful this information is, take a moment to recall the last time that any store you used to shop at did something similar to this for you. This is another way that you can provide extra-mile service for your customers — and perhaps keep them as customers.

Whether you intend to store your customer database on index cards or in a computer, you will want to track at least some of the "fields" shown in Checklist 3. This is not an exhaustive list, but it should help you identify the kind of information you would ideally like to have about each of your customers. We have included a copy of this checklist on the CD-ROM.

You may not build your database all at once — and you certainly won't get all of the information at once — but you should at least understand what you are trying to achieve and establish the basic structure. You should also decide which items you *must* know in order to conduct your relationship marketing program.

In order to build your database of customer names, addresses, and telephone numbers, you will need to get this basic information and much more from the customers themselves. The challenge is to do it without being intrusive or pushy — and without slowing your point of sale.

The ideal situation would be for each of your customers to carry a plastic card that contains a unique bar code. Each time the customer shops, you would scan first the bar code and then each of the items the person is buying that day. The challenge lies in getting your customers to carry plastic cards and present them each time they shop. This is difficult to do without an incentive.

That is why we suggest you "buy" the information from your customers by giving them several incentives that make it worth having their name in your database. You could then market these incentives together as a VIP Club and say to your customers:

> We have a VIP Club that we would like you to join. Membership offers a number of benefits, including a 5 percent discount on every regular-price item you buy in the store. You also get advance notice of our semi-annual sales and a quarterly electronic newsletter that provides helpful information about the products that we carry. Beyond this, we would like to send you a card and a small gift certificate on your birthday. Would you like to join?

If the customer says yes, you would then provide a brief application form that asks for his or her basic information: name, address, telephone number, email, and birthday. The application should also ask if the customer wants you to call them at home or at work, and at any particular time of the day. Finally, the application should provide reassurance that you will not sell or lend your mailing list to any other business — something no extra-mile retailer should ever do.

CHECKLIST 3
PREFERRED-CUSTOMER DATABASE FIELDS

Information	Format	Must know
Prefix (Mr., Ms., Dr.)	Text	
First name	Text	
Middle initial	Text	
Last name	Text	
Suffix (MD, Jr., Sr.)	Text	
Birth date	Date	
Home street address	Text	
Home city	Text	
Home state/province	Text	
Home zip/postal code	Text	
Email address	Text	
Home telephone	Number	
Calls at home?	Yes/no	
Best time to call	Time	
Mail to home?	Yes/no	
Mail to office?	Yes/no	
Work/business name	Text	
Work street address	Text	
Work city	Text	
Work state/province	Text	
Work zip/postal code	Text	
Work telephone	Number	
Calls at work?	Yes/no	
Best time to call	Time	

Information	Format	Must know
Spouse's name	Text	
Spouse's work telephone	Number	
Can call spouse?	Yes/no	
Favorite color	Text	
Size	Text	
Last purchase date	Date	
Last purchase amount	Currency	
Spouse's birth date	Date	
Spouse's favorite color	Text	
Spouse's size	Text	
Spouse's email	Text	
Wedding anniversary	Date	
Number of children	Number	
Name of child (1)	Text	
Birth date of child (1)	Date	
Name of child (2)	Text	
Birth date of child (2)	Date	
Name of child (3)	Text	
Birth date of child (3)	Date	
Other:		
Other:		
Notes	Memo	
Preferences	Memo	
Important information	Memo	

As part of this application form, you could have a detachable VIP Club Membership Card, one that contains the bar code that we mentioned earlier. The customer will be much more likely to carry the card if they get a 5 percent discount each time they shop in your store *plus* all of the other benefits of membership. You could also use a simple sticker that they place on the back of their favorite credit card so it is always handy.

As an alternative to asking your customers to carry cards or stickers, you could store them alphabetically in a box that you keep near the cash register.

However you deal with the cards, we believe you should design your VIP Club so that it rewards customer loyalty. The intention is not to give a discount to as many customers as possible. Rather, it is to give your best customers more and better services, more attention, more thanks, and more reasons to shop regularly.

These people have chosen your store as the place where they want to buy certain items. This suggests that the most appropriate reward for their loyalty would be more of those same items — perhaps a $10 gift certificate for every $100 spent in your store. These would be easy to track and easy to redeem, two things that also represent extra-mile service for your best customers.

a word to the wise

Relationship marketing can have an unexpected benefit for your business: It can literally add value to your balance sheet.

Although you may not be thinking of this now, you may someday want to sell your business. When this time comes, you can provide inventory reports and use them to negotiate a fair price for your inventory. You can also provide your balance sheet and use it to negotiate a fair price for your leasehold improvements: your fixtures, racks, and carpet.

But what about goodwill? How can you demonstrate the value of the ongoing relationships you have with your customers? A good way to prove this asset would be to provide the names, addresses, and phone numbers of every customer you have had in the past five years, complete with their purchase history by dollar volume. This could be worth literally thousands of dollars to you and to the purchaser of your business.

**put it
to work**

We suggest that you pause here to look back over the topics we have covered in this chapter on customer service. While everything is fresh in your mind, you need to decide how well prepared you are for this part of an owner-operated retailer's job.

You then need to decide what three customer service issues you can work on immediately, what three pieces of additional information you need, and which three people you should telephone or meet with soon.

How well prepared are you for customer service? (Circle one.)

READINESS		RATING
Need to hire a consultant	✐	1
Need to take some courses	✐	2
Need to read some books	✐	3
Can handle this with effort	✐	4
Can handle this in my sleep	✐	5

What three customer service issues can you work on immediately, and what can you do about each of them?

1 _____

2 _____

3 _____

What three pieces of additional information do you need to better understand the customer service part of your job?

1 _____

2 _____

3 _____

Which three people should you telephone or meet with soon about the customer service part of your job?

1 _____

2 _____

3 _____

Please transfer these answers to the Action Plan in Appendix 1.

8
THE IN-STORE EXPERIENCE

This part of your job includes:

- Stepping to the other side of the counter and giving customers what they want

- Keeping up to date in all areas and delighting the senses with something unique

- Acting like a premium brand that customers will choose as a better alternative

- Presenting merchandise as if you were telling a story, like a theater company would

- Carefully creating an environment that will encourage an emotional reaction by:

  - Dimming the house lights and putting the focus on the stage

  - Eliminating all possible distractions to preserve the magic

  - Establishing a feeling with music, in sync with the action

  - Having "actors" play specific roles for which they audition

  - Creating a huge difference between onstage and offstage

**your job
description**

Stepping to the Other Side of the Counter

In the previous seven chapters, we have looked at things mostly from the retailer's side of the counter — and that is likely what you expected from a how-to-do-it book. It is not, however, enough to make your business profitable in the long term.

After your store has been operating for about a year, you will need to step around to the other side of the counter and take a long, hard look at everything from *the customers'* perspective. You will need to start taking your real-life customers' thoughts, wishes, and dreams into account, and spend much more of your business life giving them what they want. One important way to do this is to optimize their in-store experience.

In his autobiography, *Sam Walton: Made in America*, retailer Sam Walton tells how he built Walton's Five and Dime — a 4,000-square-foot store in Bentonville, Arkansas — into Wal-Mart, the largest retailer in the world. Among many gems of retail wisdom, Sam offers his Ten Rules for Building a Business. Number eight is "Exceed your customers' expectations." "If you do, they'll come back over and over," he writes. "Give them what they want — and a little more. Let them know you appreciate them."

As we have noted previously, the retail business has changed significantly in the past 35 years. But retail customers' expectations have changed even more. They have "been there, done that, and bought the T-shirt" from some of the best companies in the world, and their expectations are much, much higher as a result.

This is partly due to things that retailers have done, partly due to advances in computer and Internet technology, and partly due to basic demographic trends. It is not as easy as it once was for an owner-operated retailer to follow Sam Walton's advice.

Retailers have changed customers' expectations by consistently introducing bigger and better retail concepts and by reducing in-store service. Customers are quite accustomed to driving to the nearest big-box store to stock up on huge quantities of same-in-every-store commodity items, including some of the most-trusted brand names in the marketplace. Many people quite happily choose self-service over full service because they have learned through experience that they can probably do things more quickly and efficiently by themselves and skip paying for mediocre service. It is now quite common for customers to expect no-frills prices even when they are shopping in a store with frills.

Computer and Internet technology have changed customers' expectations by providing what many of them have always wanted: a chance to express themselves, a way to get honest answers to their questions, and a forum in which to share their interests and passions with other customers. And these are above and beyond almost total price transparency that lets anyone find out how much a particular item should really cost. All of this means that businesses, including owner-operated retailers, need to behave very differently today than in the past. They need to let information flow freely, participate in genuine conversations with customers, and treat customers not as numbers or statistics, but as human beings.

Demographic trends have changed customers by fragmenting the marketplace. While stores used to be able to satisfy customers by being "everything to everyone," at least five demographic "cohorts" are now shopping in malls. The two most visible groups expect very different things from stores. Baby boomers have long been used to being catered to because of their sheer numbers. But in recent years, the *children* of the baby boomers have also entered the marketplace. Any retailer that tries to appeal to both older customers and people that are 30 years younger will find out that it is almost impossible to ignore the many stage-of-life issues that come into play.

All of this means that owner-operated retailers need to understand their customers better than they ever have before. Fortunately, it takes little more than structured, face-to-face conversations on the selling floor and perhaps a few focus groups to learn exactly who your customers are and what they want from your business.

If you make learning from customers a part of your regular routine — and eventually share that responsibility with the other people on your team — you will be able to optimize the in-store experience for the people who truly pay the bills and count the most.

that's a good idea

Learning from customers can be a fascinating experience. Every person who walks through the door has thoughts and feelings, a fact that often gets lost in an industry where it is all too easy to focus on transactions. As part of a consulting project he did with a resort-area gift store, Ted Topping encouraged the store's manager and staff to learn from customers by asking six customers per day one of the following pairs of questions:

1. We are thinking of making some changes to the store (do not specify). Did we have what you were looking for today?   [ ] YES   [ ] NO
   What would you like to see us carry more of? _____

2. We are thinking of making some changes to the store (do not specify). Did we have what you were looking for today?   [ ] YES   [ ] NO
   What would you like to see us do differently? _____

3. We are thinking of making some changes to the store (do not specify). Did we have what you were looking for today?   [ ] YES   [ ] NO
   How could we make your life simpler or easier? _____

It took time for the manager and staff to feel comfortable asking these questions, but eventually they were able to work them into their normal selling conversations. And as they wrote down the answers and stored them in a binder for tabulation and reference, trends started to emerge. The store rightly did not give the same weight to every customer's opinion, but it did adopt many of its customers' suggestions.

Keeping Up to Date in All Areas

Change is a fact of life in retail. Even small owner-operated retailers need to keep up to date in all areas of the business and stay in tune with what is happening in the broader retail world. Then they need to respond accordingly in a constant process of readjusting focus, rotating products, and reconnecting with customers.

But the fact that a store is staying current and adjusting its business practices is probably not something that customers will view as "change" when they walk through the door. Today's customers take that as a given — if you are going to stay in the retail game, you are going to keep up — and they expect more of a retailer than just running in a pack with others.

Instead, customers expect retailers to be leaders — to "raise the bar," create trends, and delight the senses with something unique. They want even smaller stores to show the way and offer new, fresh merchandise on every visit. And they expect retailers to establish an appropriate mood and give them a good reason to buy.

These last two items have emotional components, and they are crucial to giving customers what they want. Research has indicated that the vast majority of all purchase decisions are made precisely where the emotions reside: in the subconscious mind.

In one study, a group of customers told researchers that they always handled competing brands and compared prices at the point of purchase, but in-store observations did not bear this out. Most often, these customers did not even glance at alternatives to their prechosen brand. They simply walked to the shelf and picked up the item with no conscious thought.

If you think about this for a minute, you will see that it adds a whole new dimension to the retail business. The logic and structure that define the retail process — everything from spreadsheets to shelf allocation to scanners — merely support the emotions that rule the selling floor. This is especially true for owner-operated retailers who have no choice but to follow the best-service strategy that we discussed in Chapter 1. In the best-service arena, retail is truly a people business. And emotions drive it.

To illustrate the power of emotions in business, take a moment to recall the last time you had a bad customer-service experience at a restaurant — and note that we were able simply to assume that you have had one.

As you were leaving the restaurant, the host or hostess probably asked you how things were. Instead of offering your real opinion, you probably answered, "Fine."

Most customers leave their response at "fine" for a number of reasons. They do not want to waste time trying to fix the restaurant. They do not believe that anyone would listen to their concerns. And even if someone did listen, they do not believe that anything would change. So they say "fine" and walk out the door vowing never to return.

If the problem in this scenario did not have to do with the quality of the food or the physical setting in which it was sold — both of which are rational judgments — the problem was likely based in emotion. The server probably said or did something that resulted in the customer feeling angry, embarrassed, disappointed, frustrated, or impatient — the reasons why most customers don't come back.

Whether they are young or old, customers want a shopping experience that is comfortable for them. What they get in most retail stores, however, is something distinctly less than that.

One study of people who made purchases under $2,500 at a wide range of retail stores in the four weeks leading up to Christmas found that about half experienced some kind of problem when shopping. And when things went wrong, they really went wrong, because these people reported experiencing 2.7 problems on average.

While you might expect things like parking to be an issue during the busy Christmas season, the problems that these customers mentioned most often were difficulty finding a product due to clutter, having to wait a long time to be served, and unhelpful store employees — all things that could have been averted with a bit of planning and effort by the store manager.

Acting Like a Premium Brand That Customers Will Choose

Customers typically make up their minds about a retail store within 15 to 30 seconds of walking through the door. They judge the presentation, the atmosphere, the merchandise, the sales associates, the music, and even the smells. And they quickly decide whether they feel comfortable enough to shop — let alone feel welcome.

This makes the initial greeting a crucial part of the in-store experience for customers, especially those who are shopping at owner-operated retailers. In many ways, these retailers are like a premium brand. Customers specifically choose them as a better alternative to department stores, national chains, and big-box retailers.

And because customers consider owner-operated retailers a premium brand, they expect them to perform not just as well as other retailers, but better. When customers make comparisons, they tend to compare owner-operated retailers with high-end retailers that sell similar merchandise, not with low-end retailers. In fact, customers will tend to compare your store with the finest stores they have visited around the world or seen in magazines, on television, or on the Internet.

The best owner-operated retailers can stand up to these comparisons. They do so by focusing on delivering a consistently positive in-store experience — which really helps their business stand out in the "experience economy."

In their book *The Experience Economy: Work Is Theatre & Every Business a Stage*, B. Joseph Pine and James H. Gilmore show how successful companies — using goods as props and services as the stage — create experiences that engage customers in an inherently personal way. They explain that the reason a cup of coffee costs more at a trendy café than it does at home or at the corner diner is that the price represents the value of the entire experience for the *customer*. The customer ultimately decides what the worth of a business's product or service is. While this idea may have seemed revolutionary at first, it is now generally accepted.

As a retailer, you should always assume that your customers have experienced some of the best that retail has to offer. They have visited spas and hair salons where harpists give live performances. They have visited music stores that employ full-time disc jockeys and sporting goods stores that offer climbing walls and kayak testing canals. They have seen famous celebrities and have attended author readings and workshops in comfortable bookstores. And, of course, they have experienced in-store coffee shops, which are old news everywhere.

Nothing surprises savvy shoppers anymore. They have learned to expect more. And if you pay attention to every detail, your store can deliver that something extra.

Cirque du Soleil is a great example of a business that pays attention to every detail — and attending one of their shows is a wonderful experience. The mission of this high-energy, animal-free circus is to "invoke the imagination, provoke the senses, and evoke the emotions of people around the world." And the standard of performance is so incredibly high that audience members almost always rise to their feet, cheering and clapping at the finale.

**that's a
good idea**

Cirque du Soleil carefully creates an environment for each performance that encourages this kind of emotional reaction from customers by doing the following specific things:

- Dimming the house lights and putting the focus on the stage
- Eliminating all possible distractions to preserve the magic
- Establishing a feeling with music, in sync with the action
- Having actors play specific roles for which they audition
- Creating a huge difference between onstage and offstage

Fundamentally, these techniques are not so different from the way the best specialty retailers create an environment that encourages an emotional reaction. You may want to take the next opportunity you have to attend a show by Cirque du Soleil.

Presenting Merchandise Like a Theater Company Would

A good way to get more customers into your store is to present the merchandise as if your store were telling a story: You need to give your "performance" a beginning, a middle, and an end.

The *beginning* is the store entrance. It sets up the story, creates expectations in the customer's mind, and makes promises that the balance of the shopping experience will need to meet. With the goal of making an appropriate first impression, the entrance should say something specific: We are cool, sophisticated, cheap, or whatever the appropriate message is. Instead, many stores launch right into, "This is what we have to sell."

The entrance should also entice, hint, and tease so that customers *want* to see the wonderful things that await them inside. Display windows are especially useful because they can showcase an article, a season, or a special offering — anything that explains the quality and value of the products you carry and the wonderful shopping experience that the store offers.

The *middle* is the inside of the store. In most cases, it should start gently because most customers will need a few seconds to orient themselves after coming through the entrance. A single, clear message — a "power display," perhaps — will have a far better chance of engaging customers than will a dozen racks or fixtures cluttering the way.

Past this point, most stores should take the time to give information about their products, rather than just displaying them. If a product contains a special component or ingredient, you should provide a sample or demonstration of it. Then explain why this component or ingredient is included in the product and, most important, what it does for the customer. This gets the customer involved and lets him or her share in the sense of discovery that once was the exclusive domain of the product's manufacturer and the store's buyer.

The more customers understand that the manufacturer and the store have worked hard to offer a unique and special product, the more they will value that product. Providing information and first-hand experience is one of the best ways that an owner-operated retailer can add value.

In terms of product presentation, the best way is to lead your customers on a journey through the store. And since every good story contains small twists and surprises along the way, you should provide a visual destination at the end of every aisle. These special displays need to engage the viewer immediately, encouraging him or her to respond with, "I just have to go over there to see what that is."

The *end* of the story is the cash and wrap, the climactic finale. This area provides an opportunity to convey subtle messages without any hard selling. As well as displaying any obvious impulse items that your store may carry — think in terms of a grocery store checkout — you might want to install a television monitor somewhere above eye level to show manufacturers' demonstrations, seasonal items, or in-store specials. Customers whose minds are occupied by motion and graphics are less likely to become bored during the final step of the sale.

that's a good idea

The sales potential of each square foot of your store depends on where the customer enters the store and how he or she moves around it. The most exposed, and therefore the most valuable, space is about ten feet inside the entrance, so you should locate merchandise with a high rate of return there.

Then, because most customers turn right when they enter a store, you should allocate high profit/high volume merchandise to that area. In a smaller store, the right-hand wall near the entrance is often called the "power wall" because of its potential to produce sales.

Once you have identified the other prime areas in your store, you should place the merchandise classifications with the highest sales and gross margin rate per square foot there. In allocating merchandise classifications to areas, don't forget vertical space as well as horizontal space, because walls and fixtures have different sales potential.

Creating an Optimal Retail Environment

Once you have written the basic story that your store will tell, you need to carefully create a retail environment that will encourage the emotional reaction you want from customers. Following our theater analogy, you need to dim the house lights and put the focus on the stage.

Focus customers' attention

Different areas in your store will influence customers differently. Some are naturally more interesting in terms of sight, sound, touch, or smell, and these will engage customers accordingly. Others are more routine, the in-between areas that allow the special areas to stand out.

Apart from these natural areas, however, you need to purposely create an effective retail setting. The way to do this is to recognize and use the high-visibility areas that customers are more likely to see as they are shopping. These are called *hot spots*, and they exist in every retail setting.

If your store is open and operating, you should stand at the entrance — or at each entrance, if you have more than one — and evaluate your floor layout from the perspective that your customers see it. Departments and classifications should be clear and well defined, providing easy direction for customers who are looking for something specific. The side and rear walls should likewise be visible, and you should have lots of clear, wide aisles that make it easy for customers to move in and about.

When you have fixed anything that looked wrong from the entrance, you need to experience the store the way your customers do. Walk through the door, turn right, and follow the aisles. And as you go, notice where your eyes look naturally. These are the hot spots, and you will most likely find them just inside the store entrance, on the feature walls, at the end of every aisle, and near the cash and wrap.

Once you get used to experiencing your store the way a customer does, the hot spots tend to become obvious because they are based on the natural flow of traffic. You can use them strategically to display items that are new, seasonal, part of a collection, or even slow moving. But unless the hot spots are visible as the customers move through the store, they will be useless.

Three kinds of hot spots merit special mention:

- *Feature walls* are the walls that appear most prominent to customers when they enter the store. Depending on your store layout, any or all of your perimeter walls could be feature walls, although the wall immediately to the right of the entrance is probably the first one that customers will see.

- *Feature areas* are locations along the main traffic pattern that customers cannot avoid seeing. These include areas such as the end of a fixture that customers view head-on or walk by to get to their destination. Feature areas are typically at the front of a department, and they are perfect for displaying seasonal, popular, or coordinating items to help draw people into the department.

- *Visual displays* can be anything from a basic mannequin presentation to a widescreen plasma HDTV. These add interest to fixtures or walls and provide a destination for customers to seek out. You can use them to draw customers off the basic traffic pattern into a department or area for a closer look. The most effective displays show a product with related items in real or simulated use, helping to answer every customer's basic question: "What will it do for me?"

Using hot spots effectively will help you tell your story by directing the flow of traffic and focusing on the areas where customers will tend to stop. Signs, graphics, and lighting can help to direct your customers' eyes and lead them to where you want them to go.

Visual presentation and display is a tricky combination of science and art. Educators can describe much of the science, but the art is more difficult — and almost always achieved by someone with artistic talent. This is one aspect of the business where you may *need* to use the services of an outside professional, someone who can help you identify exactly what merchandise should be grouped together and why.

Like the scenes in a play, every display needs to tell a part of the total story of your store. You can build displays around themes such as the following:

- *Commodity or item.* Putting merchandise that is similar in one place to increase the total impact.

- *Color.* Developing color blocks so that customers see groupings of the same colors together.

- *Brand.* Creating blocks of products with the same brand name so that customers see them all in one place.

- *Price.* Grouping similar or identically priced merchandise.

- *Seasonal or special-occasion items.* Products for spring, summer, fall, winter, or occasions such as back-to-school or national and religious holidays.

Effective displays let you highlight selected merchandise while adding excitement that customers can truly feel. The secret is to keep your displays simple and straightforward, letting the products do most of the talking. Brochures or signs next to a display can give customers the rest of the information they need, including each item's name, number, and price.

Merchandise signs are silent salespeople. They help customers make informed buying decisions by adding to their knowledge of your products and services. At a more subtle level, signs also make customers feel smarter, help them make decisions faster, and let them know that they are making a good choice, thereby reducing buyer's remorse.

Research has shown that signage can make a huge difference in selling merchandise. Consider the following data:

- Adding a selling-price sign to a display can increase sales by 24 percent

- Adding a descriptive or benefit sign to regular-priced merchandise can increase sales by 33 percent

- Adding a benefit sign to sale merchandise can increase sales by 49 percent

The type of sign also makes a difference. Sales increase with the size of the sign and when a printed sign is used instead of a handwritten sign.

Eliminate all distractions

The second step in our theater analogy for building an effective in-store experience is to eliminate all possible distractions to preserve the magic. This is not something that just happens. You need to carefully plan and orchestrate your merchandise and visual presentation, taking advantage of every opportunity you have to make them more effective.

The word *distraction* can mean many things in retail settings. Ted Topping recalls a shopping trip during which he encountered quite a number of distractions in less than two hours.

Wanting to buy a pair of quick-dry casual pants, Ted went to the retail area in his city where stores specialize in outdoor apparel and equipment. At least five stores were possible sources of the particular brand name he had in mind.

In the first store, an overly friendly salesperson insisted on following Ted around, offering unsolicited personal opinions about whatever products happened to be on the rack that Ted was closest to at that moment. The only way for Ted to avoid this distraction was to leave the store, which he did. Quickly.

The second store was an old favorite where Ted had shopped several times in the past for the very item he was seeking that day. But, as fate would have it, the store was virtually devoid of apparel, apparently having decided to focus on footwear and hiking goods instead. The apparel-section walls were still there, but they were mostly empty — a sad distraction to the task at hand.

Ted then moved on to the third store, the local outlet of a small chain that promises customers a large selection of specialty products. And the store did have a large selection, including the brand name that Ted wanted. However, all of that manufacturer's products were tightly jammed onto two 4-arm feature racks, with no separation of styles, colors, sizes, or anything else. It was impossible to remove a pair of pants from the rack without causing at least one other pair to fall to the floor — something that apparently did not concern the store's two employees. They remained behind the cash and wrap, carrying on an animated conversation that frequently included the words *dude* and *awesome*. Three distractions, all in one store.

The fourth store was an outlet location for a local manufacturer and, although it did not carry the brand name that Ted had in mind, it did offer a reasonable alternative. But Ted had to discover this on his own because there was no offer of assistance from the store's staff. However, the real problems started when Ted approached the fitting rooms and found that they were blocked by about 12 large cartons, presumably that day's shipment of new merchandise. After he had moved enough cartons to get through, Ted found that the door of the fitting room did not close properly. Add more distractions to the list.

Only after visiting these four stores did Ted do what he probably should have done in the first place: He headed across the street to the member-owned, full-service retailer that seldom allows distractions of *any* kind to interfere with the in-store experience. Ted left with pants that carried a different brand name than he expected to buy that day, but his total purchase was nine items and just under $350 — any or all of which could easily have gone to the other stores if they had even remotely wanted his business. Instead, all they offered were distractions.

At a very basic level, a positive in-store experience pleases customers because they find shopping easier and more enjoyable than in other stores. At another level, it increases loyalty and repeat purchases by creating an exciting and unique shopping experience that meets or exceeds customers' expectations. The secret is to have consistency between all the forms of in-store communication: atmosphere, comfort, convenience, design, discovery, interactivity, involvement, and store cleanliness.

If, like many owner-operated retailers, you are not in a position to tackle these all at once, you can at least start with the fundamentals:

- Position the fixtures in your store based on traffic flow and sight-lines. You should place them where they will not impede traffic flow, allowing customers to move freely throughout the store. At the same time, fixtures should not block sightlines to other parts of the store or create hidden areas that encourage shoplifting.

- Present the most important merchandise at eye level, the optimum height that lets customers scan it visually. Customers will not buy what they do not see, so you need to place the high-profit articles where they *will* be noticed — and make sure you aim appropriate lighting directly at them.

a word to the wise

Lighting is a tool; just like any tool, how you use it determines whether it will have a positive or negative effect. Bad lighting may actually give customers the wrong impression of your store and the products you offer.

That said, good lighting does not necessarily mean more lighting. It takes an investment of time, money, and people to have effective and efficient lighting in a retail store, but once you understand the many benefits that it offers, you will see that it is an investment you really should make.

Lighting creates an atmosphere in the store and powerfully affects customers' perceptions of the business, its products, and its quality of service. An emphasis on overhead lighting can create the feeling of a discount retailer, while an emphasis on accent lighting can create the feeling of a high-end specialty store.

Establish a feeling with music

Because a customer's decision to purchase is based largely on emotional responses, savvy retailers work hard at the third step in our theater analogy for building an effective in-store experience: Establish a feeling with music in sync with the action.

Thirty-five years ago, only large retailers could afford to worry about the music they played in their stores. Owner-operated retailers had little choice but to play whatever FM radio station seemed the most appropriate — commercials, newscasts, and all. Talk about distractions!

In the age of digital music, it no longer has to be that way. Smaller retailers now can also take advantage of specially selected music, which is one of the most powerful ways of helping customers feel confident and comfortable in a retail environment.

Music does this by providing informational clues about the uniqueness of a store's merchandise and level of service. Music establishes a mood, helps motivate the subconscious, and creates a lasting impression. Used properly, music can be an important tool for establishing a retail brand's identity in the minds of customers. At the very least, it has the potential to increase or decrease a customer's satisfaction with the shopping experience.

Many customers are not even aware of the music that retail stores — and office buildings, restaurants, and most other public places — play. But it can nonetheless be connecting powerfully with specific target markets by reflecting customer demographics such as age, gender mix, and income levels, as well as psychographics such as personality, preferences, lifestyles, and attitudes.

All of this might make it sound like selecting music that will enhance your customer's in-store experience is a complicated matter. And it is. Music is as much a job for professionals as store design or visual merchandising — all are beyond the scope of the average retailer.

If you can possibly afford it, you should have a long conversation with a company that supplies music to retail businesses. You will learn about things such as "performance rights," and that no business can legally use a consumer broadcast of any kind as background music unless it pays a licensing fee. The same rules apply to digital music. The fee you pay to download a song from the Internet does *not* give you the right to play that song to customers over the sound system in your store.

One of the more intriguing sources of appropriate in-store music is satellite radio. It offers a broad range of commercial-free music programs in many genres, and the suppliers all sell packages that are appropriate for businesses. Satellite radio also lets you try an interesting experiment: At the flick of a switch, you can "color" your store with the soft, soothing sounds of the easy-listening channel, the rough, edgy sounds of the blues channel, or the driving, pulsing sounds of the hip-hop channel. Whatever effect you want, it is likely available commercial free on satellite radio.

A writer for a national magazine once offered an interesting look at the use of music in retail when he interviewed a creative manager at Muzak, the company that supplies 60 percent of the commercial background music in the United States. This person's job is to create programs specifically for Muzak clients, one of which is a popular-price fashion retailer.

"Shoppers there are looking for clothes that are hip and chic and cool," she explained. "They are 25 to 35 years old, they want something to wear to a party or a club and, as they shop, they want to feel like they are already there. So you make the store sound like the coolest bar in town. You think about that when you pick the songs and you pay special attention to the sequencing. You cross fade and beat match, never breaking the momentum, because you want the program to sound like a DJ's mix."*

A well-known lingerie chain also uses music to enhance the in-store experience. Playing classical music has contributed to a store atmosphere that implies prestige. This, in turn, has led to a widespread customer perception that the company offers high-quality merchandise and service.

As these examples suggest, in-store music should carefully reflect the profile of your primary target customer and the products that you carry in the store. In most cases, it should be played at a fairly low volume so that your customers and your sales associates can have the two-way conversations that *must* take place uninterrupted in a best-service strategy store. In other words, the music in your store is crucially important, but it has to be just one more manifestation of something so familiar that we scarcely notice it: the shifting and frequently inescapable soundtrack of everyday life.

---

* David Owen, "The Soundtrack of Your Life," *The New Yorker*, April 10, 2006.

An international bookseller designs its stores as warm, relaxing, and pleasant gathering places — a strategy designed to maximize the length of time that people spend in the store. Customers are encouraged to relax, choose three or four books from the enormous selection available, sit down and enjoy a coffee or some food, perhaps take in some music, and basically just while away the hours.

that's a good idea

Even the in-store music is designed to maximize the length of a customer's visit. Research has shown that if shoppers stay longer and travel more slowly through the store, they probably will purchase more. The tempo of the music at these stores is slow and relaxed, and it tends to alter a customer's perception of the passing of time. Shoppers and sales associates also report that the soothing music helps to facilitate conversations about the store's products and services.

Have professional sales associates play their roles

Some owner-operated retailers feel uncomfortable with the fourth step in our theater analogy for creating an effective in-store experience: Have actors play specific roles for which they audition. Perhaps it is our use of the verb *play*, or the thought of sales associates performing *roles* instead of simply being themselves. In any case, some retailers start to dig in their heels, not understanding that this reaction is self-defeating since the people side of the business is by far the most crucial element in giving customers what they want.

We are not really saying anything new here. If you think back to Chapter 4, you will recall that we recommended giving all of your employees the job title of sales associate because it denotes a true professional and describes not what your people are, but what they are supposed to do and how they are supposed to do it.

By definition, a *professional* is someone who shows a high degree of skill or competence and is engaged in an occupation as a paid job rather than as a hobby. In retail, these people find a way to leave their personal lives and problems behind them when they walk onto the selling floor. They focus instead on the needs of the customers that they are paid to satisfy. When you think of it in that way, every professional in every industry is an actor who is playing a specific role.

Professional sales associates who possess superior selling skills can often help a retail store overcome whatever shortcomings it may have. Certainly their personal, one-on-one interaction with a customer will always be the most tangible and memorable part of that customer's in-store experience.

Since we wrote the first edition of this book, we have come to believe that *suggestion selling* is both the most important part of a sales associate's duties and the single best way to differentiate a best-service-strategy retailer from competitors that focus on greatest assortment and lowest price.

Some people will tell you that closing sales is what counts the most in full-service retail, but we think that it is suggestion selling — which should be at least 35 percent of a sales associate's focus and more than twice as important as anything else that he or she does.

We say this knowing that many things need to happen before a sales associate can reach that step of the sale. He or she needs to establish contact with the customer and then engage that person in a wide-ranging conversation in which the sales associate asks questions and listens, while the customer talks. As this is happening, the sales associate needs to mentally search for the product that best meets the customer's needs — and think of all the related items that would complete the purchase and increase the customer's overall satisfaction. That is what a professional sales associate does.

This is also why many customers choose to patronize an owner-operated retailer instead of one of the many self-service alternatives that are available in today's highly competitive marketplace. Sales associates need to understand the importance and effectiveness of suggestion selling. If a customer walks out of the store with just one item, the sales associate may not have performed effectively.

Another way that sales associates can optimize the in-store experience for customers is by adjusting their selling approach based on the gender of the customer. Although it is always dangerous to generalize, research tends to support the observation that women and men have quite different attitudes toward shopping and that they shop in very different ways. The broad-brush statement is that women enjoy shopping while men do not.

Certainly, women tend to browse stores, while men tend to do it only in stores that sell particular products. For the most part, women are more interested in reading product brochures, care instructions, and comparison charts. They are also more concerned about who serves them and how they are treated. Most female customers want to feel comfortable about a sales associate's genuine interest in their needs before they want to hear any product information.

Men, on the other hand, find shopping a bit overwhelming, according to a British psychologist who looked at the stress levels of 36 people that he sent Christmas shopping. In that study, researchers with portable monitoring equipment accompanied people of both genders as they looked for specific gift items.

One of four women in the study exhibited an elevated heart rate and increased blood pressure, while *every* man had *significant* increases in these stress indicators. In fact, some men had peak levels equivalent to those of fighter pilots in emergency situations or policemen in dangerous circumstances. The men reported that they were likely to choose the first gift they saw rather than spend any more time in a store than absolutely necessary.

These results suggest that it may be very helpful to "test shop" your store using both male and female shoppers — friends, family, or volunteer customers who are willing to offer feedback — to see if they react differently to in-store variables such as feature walls, visual displays, lighting, signs, music, or the customer service that your sales associates provide.

a word to the wise

For many owner-operated retailers, the challenge today is not so much finding professional sales associates as it is finding *anyone* to work in the business.

The lack of workers that many employers now face is rooted in the fact that almost one of every three North Americans was born during the post-war baby boom — approximately 81 million people in the U.S. and 10 million people in Canada. When these people were in their prime child-producing years, they did not produce the slightly more than two children that it would have taken to replace themselves in the population. This led to there being just 70 million children of the baby boomers in the U.S. and 7 million in Canada — and to both countries now facing a shortage of the younger workers that have traditionally filled entry-level positions.

Hiring a 20-year-old for an entry-level position was a good recruiting strategy 35 years ago, but it is not very effective today. More and more employers are competing for fewer and fewer candidates. And the worst is yet to come, since 20-year-olds will represent an ever smaller portion of the total population in each of the years ahead. For many employers, a better strategy is to look for people with more life and work experience.

A huge number of experienced and capable people in their 40s and 50s are currently available to employers due to the cutbacks and downsizing of the 1990s and the outsourcing of jobs to less-expensive parts of the world more recently. There is, however, a catch.

These are not entry-level employees in the traditional sense. Carefully chosen, they can add immeasurably to any team, providing a valuable balance to younger workers. But getting and keeping them will require most business owners to rethink the fundamental way in which they run the people side of their operations.

Differentiate onstage and offstage areas

The fifth step in creating a retail environment that encourages the emotional reaction you want from customers is the step that will bring you closest to the world of theater. You need to create a huge difference between *onstage* and *offstage*.

For members of a theater audience, a "backstage pass" is a coveted possession. It can provide access to a private reception, with a chance to meet the artists, or perhaps just a few moments of standing alone on an empty stage, listening to the applause of an imaginary audience. In their A Bigger Bang world tour of 2005–06, The Rolling Stones acknowledged this kind of interest on the part of their fans when they sold tickets to special "standing room" boxes on the stage for a considerable price.

People value these kinds of experiences because they briefly lift the curtain and provide a glimpse of what it takes to create the magic that makes up each performance. Said another way, these experiences let people cross the line between onstage and offstage.

In the theater world, backstage passes are very rare. In the retail world, they should not exist at all. The only thing that any customer should *ever* experience is the onstage magic.

The onstage elements of retail are the exterior, the display windows, the store entrance, the selling space, and anywhere else that is designed for the customer. This is where everything that we have described in this chapter comes together in support of the sales associates who sell and deliver good customer service.

The offstage elements are the behind-the-scenes areas where customers do not go. These include the store's stockroom, its shipping and receiving facilities, its offices and lunchroom, and all of the mechanical equipment. These are the areas where sales associates can act and speak freely, where they can do their research and prepare themselves for work.

As the authors of this book, we are sometimes invited to participate as guests on radio or television programs. The most enjoyable of these let us speak live on the air with people who care enough about something to call in and share their thoughts with tens of thousands of listeners. Without doubt, the retail topic that callers want to discuss the most is customer service. We have heard a few positive stories along the way, but most people want to vent about the retail clerk who was too busy unpacking boxes to even say hello, let alone answer questions. Or the one who was cleaning mirrors so intently that she did not notice that two customers were being ignored. Or the one who turned his back on everyone and everything in the store and chatted on the phone with a friend.

These customers probably believed that they were angry with a retail clerk, but really they were angry because an activity that should have been conducted offstage somehow got onstage. And it totally destroyed any magic that the store may have held for that customer.

The biggest reason to keep onstage and offstage areas separated is that anything that does not support and enhance the in-store experience will, by definition, detract from it. Equally important, sales associates *need* an offstage area where they can go to eat and relax when they are not working. It is the only way that they can be professional when they *are* working onstage.

Separating your onstage and offstage areas may take some careful planning. Smells and sounds in particular have a way of traveling from the offstage area directly to a customer's nose and ears. You *must* find a way to eliminate this kind of distraction if you want to create an in-store experience that is always extraordinary.

Although Volkswagen is hardly an owner-operated retailer, the largest producer of automobiles in Europe presents a wonderful example of the way that theater can be used in retail. Its unique Autostadt in Wolfsburg, Germany, allows customers to learn about trends in the automobile industry as well as select their new vehicles. Over 10,000 automobiles are available for display and customer pickup, each one of which is washed, vacuumed, cleaned, and put through a quality-control inspection on site. Once a vehicle is perfect, it is raised into one of two 20-story glass towers.

For a customer, collecting a new car in the Autostadt is a true theatrical event. In a fully automated procedure, a pneumatic lift brings your new car down from its storage location. Large signboards in the Customer Center advise you when your turn has come. Then you are handed the keys, your picture is taken, the glass doors open, and your brand-new car appears.

Is all of this absolutely necessary? No. Does it make the purchase of a new car special? Beyond anything you have ever seen — which is exactly what you, as an owner-operated retailer, need to do with the products you sell.

**put it
to work**

We suggest that you pause here to look back over the topics we have covered in this chapter on the in-store experience. While everything is fresh in your mind, you need to decide how well prepared you are for this part of an owner-operated retailer's job.

You then need to decide what three in-store experience issues you can work on immediately, what three pieces of additional information you need, and which three people you should telephone or meet with soon.

How well prepared are you for the in-store experience? (Circle one.)

READINESS		RATING
Need to hire a consultant	✏	1
Need to take some courses	✏	2
Need to read some books	✏	3
Can handle this with effort	✏	4
Can handle this in my sleep	✏	5

What three in-store experience issues can you work on immediately and what can you do about each of them?

1_____

2_____

3_____

What three pieces of additional information do you need to understand the in-store experience part of your job?

1_____

2_____

3_____

Which three people you should telephone or meet with soon about the in-store experience part of your job?

1_____

2_____

3_____

Please transfer these answers to the Action Plan in Appendix 1.

AFTERWORD

As we said in the introduction, we believe that you stand a good chance of starting and running a profitable retail business if you are prepared to follow the steps outlined in this book, learn your craft, and become a professional retailer. While reading the intervening pages, however, you may have become a bit discouraged.

You may feel reasonably comfortable with some parts of the job description that we have presented, but downright uncomfortable with other parts. For example, you may feel reasonably comfortable with human resources but uncomfortable with technology. This is both normal and natural, since everyone has strengths and weaknesses.

The challenge now facing you is to build your business idea around your strengths while drawing selectively on the skills of other people to compensate for your weaknesses. Every part of your job is important, but that does not imply you should try to do everything yourself. On the contrary, we believe that you should try to build a solid team that includes employees, suppliers, and the other "partners" in your business.

A good way to start is to focus now on the Put It to Work sections at the end of each chapter. If you have not done so already, you should take time to decide how well prepared you are for the eight sections of your job description. Are you ready to handle each one? Or do you perhaps need to read some books, take some courses, or even hire a consultant to help you?

Next you need to start moving from where you are now to where you want to go — but you should not do this haphazardly. Instead, you should identify the issues that you can work on immediately, obtain the additional information that you require, and telephone or meet with people who can help you move forward. If you take these steps, you will find yourself making progress almost before you know it. The appendixes that follow should really support you in this regard.

Appendix 1 helps you create a unique action plan for the next few months. If you treat this as a checklist and work through it line by line, you will see yourself making genuine progress as the weeks go by. This can be very encouraging when the going gets rough, as it inevitably will.

Appendix 2 gives you a list of books that expand — some directly and some indirectly — on the topics we have presented. We encourage every owner-operated retailer to become a "student of retail." This means keeping up with the latest trends by reading books, trade publications, and articles on the Internet. It also means joining associations, attending workshops, and networking as often as possible with people from whom you can learn.

The CD-ROM that accompanies this book provides a complete set of forms and worksheets from this book that you can print out and use to plan your new business. We believe that you should put a lot of time and effort into completing these forms and worksheets because there is absolutely no point in investing anything more than this until you can make your business work on paper. You may be tempted to move on to the "fun stuff" instead of working through the budgets, but we suggest that you avoid the temptation.

If you decide after reading this book that becoming an owner-operated retailer is the investment and career choice that is right for you, we wish you every success in your new business.

And if you have thoughts, opinions, or comments about *Start and Run a Retail Business* that you would like to share with the authors — either before or after you open your store — we invite you to contact us through our websites, or c/o Self-Counsel Press at the addresses shown in the front of the book.

You can learn more about Jim Dion by visiting www.dionco.com. You can learn more about Ted Topping by visiting www.tedtopping.com.

APPENDIX 1

PUT IT TO WORK: ACTION PLAN

How ready are you to juggle the eight different parts of the job description of an owner-operated retailer? Transfer your answers from the end of each chapter, and then use the following table to help evaluate your readiness to start and run a profitable retail business.

	Need to hire a consultant	Need to take some courses	Need to read some books	Can handle this with effort	Can handle this in my sleep
Chapter 1: The basics of retail	1	2	3	4	5
Chapter 2: Merchandising	1	2	3	4	5
Chapter 3: Buying	1	2	3	4	5
Chapter 4: Human resources	1	2	3	4	5
Chapter 5: Sales management	1	2	3	4	5
Chapter 6: Technology	1	2	3	4	5
Chapter 7: Customer service	1	2	3	4	5
Chapter 8: The in-store experience	1	2	3	4	5

What issues can you work on immediately and what can you do about each of them? Transfer your answers from the end of each chapter, and then use the following checklist to help mark your progress toward starting and running a profitable retail business.

Chapter 1: The basics of retail   Completed

1 _____ ☐

2 _____ ☐

3 _____ ☐

Chapter 2: Merchandising

1 _____ ☐

2 _____ ☐

3 _____ ☐

Chapter 3: Buying

1 _____ ☐

2 _____ ☐

3 _____ ☐

Chapter 4: Human resources

1 _____ ☐

2 _____ ☐

3 _____ ☐

Chapter 5: Sales management

1 _____ ☐

2 _____ ☐

3 _____ ☐

Chapter 6: Technology

1 _____ ☐

2 _____ ☐

3 _____ ☐

Chapter 7: Customer service

1 _____ ☐

2 _____ ☐

3 _____ ☐

Chapter 8: The in-store experience

1 _____ ❏

2 _____ ❏

3 _____ ❏

What additional information do you need to better understand each part of your job? Transfer your answers from the end of each chapter, and then use the following checklist to help mark your progress toward starting and running a profitable retail business.

Chapter 1: The basics of retail   Completed

1 _____ ❏

2 _____ ❏

3 _____ ❏

Chapter 2: Merchandising

1 _____ ❏

2 _____ ❏

3 _____ ❏

Chapter 3: Buying

1 _____ ❏

2 _____ ❏

3 _____ ❏

Chapter 4: Human resources

1 _____ ❏

2 _____ ❏

3 _____ ❏

Chapter 5: Sales management

1 _____ ❏

2 _____ ❏

3 _____ ❏

Chapter 6: Technology

1 _____ ❏

2 _____ ❏

3 _____ ❏

Chapter 7: Customer service

1 _____ ❑

2 _____ ❑

3 _____ ❑

Chapter 8: The in-store experience

1 _____ ❑

2 _____ ❑

3 _____ ❑

Which three people should you telephone or meet with soon to discuss the different parts of your job? Transfer your answers from each chapter, and then use the following checklist to help mark your progress toward starting and running a profitable retail business.

Chapter 1: The basics of retail   Completed

1 _____ ❑

2 _____ ❑

3 _____ ❑

Chapter 2: Merchandising

1 _____ ❑

2 _____ ❑

3 _____ ❑

Chapter 3: Buying

1 _____ ❑

2 _____ ❑

3 _____ ❑

Chapter 4: Human resources

1 _____ ❑

2 _____ ❑

3 _____ ❑

Chapter 5: Sales management

1 _____ ❑

2 _____ ❑

3 _____ ❑

Chapter 6: Technology

1 _____ ❏

2 _____ ❏

3 _____ ❏

Chapter 7: Customer service

1 _____ ❏

2 _____ ❏

3 _____ ❏

Chapter 8: The in-store experience

1 _____ ❏

2 _____ ❏

3 _____ ❏

APPENDIX 2
ADDITIONAL READING

We believe that *Start and Run a Retail Business* should be just the beginning of your studies as a student of retail. Any of the following books will build on the foundation we have laid.

Berry, Leonard. *On Great Service: A Framework for Action.* New York: Free Press, 2006.

Blanchard, Kenneth, and Spencer Johnson. *The One Minute Manager.* New York: Berkley Books, 1983.

Collins, James C., and Jerry I. Porras. *Built to Last: Successful Habits of Visionary Companies.* New York: HarperBusiness, 2002.

Connellan, Tom. *Inside the Magic Kingdom: Seven Keys to Disney's Success.* Austin: Bard Press, 1997.

Dion, James E. *Retail Selling Ain't Brain Surgery, It's Twice As Hard.* Chicago: Dionco Inc., 2006.

Disney Institute. *Be Our Guest: Perfecting the Art of Customer Service.* New York: Disney Editions, 2001.

Falk, Edgar A. *1001 Ideas to Create Retail Excitement (Revised Edition).* New York: Prentice Hall, 2003.

Foot, David K., and Daniel Stoffman. *Boom, Bust & Echo 2000: Profiting from the Demographic Shift in the New Millenium.* Toronto: Stoddart, 2000.

Girard, Joe, with Stanley H. Brown. *How to Sell Anything to Anybody.* New York: Fireside, 2006.

Glen, Peter. *It's Not My Department: How America Can Return to Excellence — Giving and Receiving Quality Service.* New York: Berkley, 2002.

Jennings, Jason. *Think Big, Act Small: How America's Best Performing Companies Keep the Start-up Spirit Alive.* New York: Portfolio, 2005.

Johnson, Spencer. *The One Minute Sales Person: The Quickest Way to Sell People on Yourself, Your Services, Products, or Ideas — At Work and in Life (Revised Edition).* New York: William Morrow, 2002.

Jones, Patricia, and Larry Kahaner. *Say It and Live It.* New York: Doubleday, 1995.

Kabachnick, Terri. *I Quit, But Forgot to Tell You.* Largo, FL: The Kabachnick Group, 2006.

O'Dell, Susan M., and Joan A. Pajunen. *The Butterfly Customer: Capturing the Loyalty of Today's Elusive Customer (Revised Edition).* Toronto: John Wiley and Sons Canada, 2000.

Peppers, Don, and Martha Rodgers. *The One to One Future: Building Relationships One Customer at a Time.* New York: Doubleday, 1996.

Pine, B. Joseph, and James H. Gilmore. *The Experience Economy: Work Is Theatre & Every Business a Stage.* Boston: Harvard Business School Press, 1999.

Ries, Al, and Laura Ries. *The 22 Immutable Laws of Branding: How to Build a Product or Service into a World-Class Brand.* New York: HarperBusiness, 2002.

Schultz, Howard, and Dorl Jones Yang. *Pour Your Heart Into It: How Starbucks Built a Company One Cup at a Time.* New York: Hyperion, 1999.

Spector, Robert, and Patrick D. McCarthy. *The Nordstrom Way: The Inside Story of America's #1 Customer Service Company.* New York: John Wiley and Sons, 1995.

Taylor, Don, and Jeanne Smalling Archer. *Up Against the Wal-Marts: How Your Business Can Prosper in the Shadow of the Retail Giants (2nd Edition).* New York: AMACOM, 2005.

Underhill, Paco. *Why We Buy: The Science of Shopping.* New York: Simon & Schuster, 2000.

Walton, Sam, with John Huey. *Sam Walton: Made in America.* New York: Bantam Books, 1993.

Wolf, Michael. *The Entertainment Economy: How Mega-Media Forces Are Transforming Our Lives.* New York: Three Rivers Press, 2003.

Zemke, Ron, and Kristin Anderson. *Delivering Knock Your Socks Off Service (4th Edition).* New York: AMACOM, 2006.

The following worksheets are included on the enclosed CD-ROM for use on a Windows-based PC. Some forms are in MS Word and PDF formats; others are in Excel.

The Basics of Retail (Chapter 1)

- Pro forma profit and loss statement
- Volume calculator
- Developing your secret weapon
- Developing a clear vision
- Analyzing your competitors
- Location calculator
- Advertising plan

Merchandising (Chapter 2)

- Monthly maintained margin report
- Maintained margin worksheet
- Promotional markdown list
- Regular markdown laundry list
- Supplier checklist

Buying (Chapter 3)

- Six-month merchandise plan

Human Resources (Chapter 4)

- Job description of a sales associate
- Sales associate interview guide (Bonus guide for CD)
- Job interview evaluation checklist

Sales Management (Chapter 5)

- Weekly payroll budget

Technology (Chapter 6)

- Checklist for retail software
- POS software questions for retailers
- Questions for potential POS software suppliers
- Balance of business calculator

Customer Service (Chapter 7)

- Customer experience scorecard
- Evaluate your extra-mile service
- Preferred-customer database fields

Bonus Spreadsheets for Operating Retailers

- Monthly sales worksheet
- Cash flow budget planner (six month)
- Productivity ratios